MORTGAGE BROKING MASTERY

The Unconventional Playbook to Purchasing Trail Books, Scaling and Profit Boosting

THE ULTIMATE GUIDE FOR EVERY MORTGAGE BROKER

NATASHA MENON

First published by Ultimate World Publishing 2025
Copyright © 2025 Natasha Menon

ISBN

Paperback: 978-1-923255-85-2
Ebook: 978-1-923255-86-9

Cover design: Ultimate World Publishing
Layout and typesetting: Ultimate World Publishing
Editor: Carmela Julian Valencia

Ultimate World Publishing
Diamond Creek,
Victoria Australia 3089
www.writeabook.com.au

Testimonials

'The content you posted today is the best thing I've seen on Linkedin for some time, thank you'
- D.C. (Director in Melbourne, VIC)

'Your content is really valuable and easy to read. Please keep sharing!'
- M.C (Founder and Expert Lending Adviser in Greater Sydney, NSW)

'I read your post on valuing trail for mortgage brokers and thought you were spot on. Well done! I'd encourage you keep posting such excellent content'
- P.K (Franchise Accountant in Sydney, NSW)

'Her ability to develop and share insights into business performance is invaluable, making her a key contributor to the team's success. She is also a natural connector, fostering strong relationships across the organisation and with business partners.'
- B.M. (CEO, Finance at Mortgage Broking Training Institute in Melbourne, VIC)

'Natasha shows great skill and determination in all her work endeavours. Her attention to detail and solid grasp of finance and data principles ensure quality work, combined with the ability to be analytical and draw relevant insights.'

- D.M (Co-Founder of a Financing company that funded over $4 Billion in Commercial, asset and residential finance and 10,000 + Property and Business Transactions in Melbourne, Sydney and Brisbane)

'Natasha is your consummate professional, adept at tackling complex needs, identifying business drivers, and taking action to deliver outcomes. Natasha approaches her role with a growth mindset, striving for excellence whilst always transparent and accountable'

- P.G. (Mortgage Broker and Mentor in Melbourne, VIC)

'I love your articles'

- C.R (Partnership Manager at a SME Lender, Melbourne, VIC)

'I checked out your profile and I love what you're doing!'

- H.S. (High Performance Coach in Sunshine Coast, QLD)

'I will share with my brokers over email it is great for them'

- E.M (State Director, Adelaide, SA)

'Loved the article on EBITDA. Would love to unpack this more and discuss book multiples'

- R.S JP (Finance Broker, Bowral, NSW)

'Thanks for your valuable article on purchasing a trail book'

- M.R (Finance Specialist and Business Restructuring Advisor, Melbourne, VIC)

'Great article you wrote re Ryanair! I would welcome an opportunity to discuss our business'

- P.A (Commercial Finance Broker, Speaker and Mentor, Melbourne, VIC)

'If there's one sentence that could summarise Tash and a sentence that I frequently used, 'she's the smartest of us all'.'

- S.R (Banking and Finance Broking Professional in Melbourne, VIC)

Dedication

Most importantly to Jesus, whose love and grace inspire me to serve others selflessly just as I have been blessed with divine helpers along my own journey. My faith has driven me to share this knowledge selflessly in the hope that it helps mortgage brokers succeed and protects small businesses from unforeseen challenges.

To my family for being a blessing and giving me a life of no lack.

To all the mortgage brokers who have taken the leap of faith, leaving behind a stable income to build their own business and have the freedom to spend more time with their families, this book is for you. It is inspiring how much you support each other and your communities. It is time you are equally supported as you make every Australian's dream of owning a home a reality. This is my tribute to you for welcoming me in this industry with open arms. You know who you are.

For those who never stop learning and have taught me, this book is for you. To all my past and present managers and colleagues, thank you for your love and kindness and for the generous lessons and insights that helped shape this book.

Disclaimer

The content of this book is based on the author's personal experiences and observations during her time working in the mortgage broking industry. The views and opinions expressed are solely those of the author and do not represent the positions, strategies or policies of any previous employer(s) including Australasia's largest mortgage aggregator. This book is intended for educational purposes only and should not be used as a substitute for professional financial, legal or business advice. The author assumes no liability for any decisions or actions taken based on the information provided in this book.

Chapters

Introduction   1

**Section 1: Understanding the Basics of
Mortgage Broking**

A fun and simple guide to becoming a master
mortgage broker   5

From PAYG to self-employed: Understanding the
costs of becoming a mortgage broker   15

Commission vs. PAYG mortgage brokers:
Finding the best model for your business   25

From PAYG to self-employed mortgage broker:
Navigating the transition with confidence   31

Creating your value proposition:
The key to standing out as a mortgage broker   41

Recap of Section 1:
Understanding the basics of mortgage broking   51

Section 2: The Power of Trail Books

Boosting the value of your trail book   55

Getting the right price: Understanding the
valuation multiple for your trail book   61

The strategic advantage: Why buying a trail
book is a smart move for brokers   67

Cracking the code: Common and uncommon
ways to value your trail book   73

Buying a trail book: A simple guide for
new brokers   79

Mastering the art of selling your trail book:
Get the best price   85

Avoiding the pitfalls: A broker's guide to
buying a trail book the smart way   93

How to grow profits with old trail books   103

Mastering trail book acquisition: The seven-step
blueprint for mortgage brokers   109

Making an offer for a trail book: Six key points
every mortgage broker must address   117

The three-step communication strategy
for seamless trail book integration   125

Financing the trail book purchase:
What you need to know   131

Understanding TOFA's impact on trail book
purchases for mortgage brokers   137

Avoiding buyer's remorse: Common complaints
when purchasing trail books   143

Recap of Section 2: Power of trail books   150

Section 3: Mastering Financial Health

Brokerage's finances: A simple and strategic
chart of accounts   157

Why must you prioritise net profit over gross
revenue?   167

Mastering EBITDA: Key to understanding your
brokerage's financial health   173

Full valuation of your brokerage: The power of
EBITDA in business sales   181

Paying yourself as a mortgage broker:
Navigating pre-drawings vs. post-drawings   189

Maximising tax benefits for mortgage brokers:
Navigating small business concessions   199

Bucket company strategies: The smart tax
move for mortgage brokers   205

Boosting profits: Smart strategies for mortgage
brokers to maximise operating income   213

Chapter 28: Lessons from Ryanair:
How mortgage brokers can grow profits   221

Recap of Section 3: Mastering financial health   227

Section 4: Building, Expanding and Scaling Your Brokerage

Scaling smart: When and how to add staff
to your mortgage brokerage   233

Building a sales-driven culture: Essential
selling skills across every role in your brokerage   241

Mastering mentorship for mortgage brokers:
Unlocking your full potential   249

Tailored commission splits and support models
for retaining mortgage brokers   259

Navigating contracts, contractor splits and
broker agreements in mortgage broking   267

Unlocking the potential: Why hiring experienced
brokers after selling their businesses can
transform your brokerage   275

Recap of Section 4: Building, expanding and
scaling your brokerage   281

Section 5: Practical Advice for Managing Day-to-Day Operations

Prepping for a prosperous new year: Year-end essentials for mortgage brokers   285

Benchmarking: The secret to staying ahead in mortgage broking   291

Maximising the value of trail commissions in your mortgage brokerage   299

Protecting your mortgage brokerage: Five essential insurance policies to reduce risk   305

Recap of Section 5: Practical advice for managing day-to-day operations   312

Afterword   315

About the Author – Natasha Menon   317

Speaker Bio   319

Introduction

Welcome to a world where over 19,000 mortgage brokers dominate 76% of the home loan market in Australia. In a space so competitive, you can't afford to focus solely on writing loans anymore. Compliance demands, rising operational costs and the need for smart business acumen are reshaping the mortgage broking industry.

I have worked in distinct but interconnected arms of the broader financial services industry – namely, accounting, superannuation, financial planning, wealth management and mortgage broking, of course – and I haven't seen any other finance professional as handsomely rewarded, getting personal satisfaction in their job and having the work–life flexibility that mortgage brokers do.

During my time working at Australasia's largest aggregator, I was privileged to gain an insider's perspective on what separates top brokers from the rest. I am a big observer and I sponge at every opportunity. Through attending peer group sessions, one-on-one profit meetings and business strategy sessions with key players analysing financials from the billion-dollar brokers down to the industry newcomers, I had a front-row seat to loads of stories of both success and failure. I learned that multimillion-dollar success in this industry doesn't happen by chance. It's about building genuine and lasting relationships with your employees and clients and keeping it consistent.

For a couple of years now, I have been writing LinkedIn articles and reaching out to as many mortgage broker business owners as I can. Posts and articles tend to get lost, and it was time to piece them together into one cohesive strategy book. I have consolidated years of hands-on experience, behind-the-scenes insights and strategies that separate successful brokers from those who struggle.

My work life has centred around money. I appreciate the fact that it gives people the ability and financial freedom to live a life of dignity. Hence, I want to share entrepreneurial lessons to those who may not get the opportunity to learn from the super successful brokers and business owners like I do. In this book, I'll share the lessons learned from some of the most successful brokers in the business and how you can apply these strategies to grow your own brokerage. The lessons are aggregator-agnostic and timeless.

This is a guide designed to empower you with everything you need to know besides purely generating leads. Whether you're just starting out or looking to grow your business, these are the topics you need to be aware of and consider. I hope this book gives you the tools and confidence to thrive.

To those who mentor, educate and provide sales support to your brokers, this is the perfect gift. Hand it to someone looking at mortgage broking as a business, not a job. This thoughtful and respectful book explains why they need to work on the business, not in it, while honouring their intellect. It is a culmination of years of experience and a passion for helping all mortgage brokers without bias.

CHAPTER 1

A fun and simple guide to becoming a master mortgage broker

Sadie, a loan processor from Queensland, worked for a broker for under two years, doing the behind-the-scenes work. She would watch the Head Broker (similar age as hers) breeze into meetings with clients, make deals and walk out to record her podcast. Sadie figured, 'I could do that. How hard could it be?' After all, she knew the products inside out, had client files organised and was a gen Z full of charm.

One day Sadie, took the plunge, left her admin job and started her own brand. Soon, reality hit hard. In her first few weeks, the phone wasn't ringing and clients didn't come knocking. She felt invisible.

When she came in for a coaching session, she realised the secret wasn't product knowledge but relationships. The head broker whom she worked for wasn't recording podcasts to get famous on Spotify but to cultivate a community of trust.

Sadie took a deep breath and decided to change her approach as we recommended. She started connecting with referral partners, building relationships that went both ways by sending leads back to them too. Slowly but surely, over 18 months, things began to change. Her brand reputation grew and so did her business.

You may be working as a banker or doing the admin for a mortgage broker. You see the mortgage broker spending time with clients and leaving all the boring administrative tasks to you. You think even you can do that, but you forget the journey it is to get to that stage. Becoming a successful mortgage broker requires more than just an understanding of a few financial products. It is about having a community that trusts you and comes to you for finance, time and time again. Whether you're a seasoned broker or just getting started, there are essential strategies that can set you up for long-term success in this competitive yet rewarding field. Here's a breakdown of some key principles to keep in mind as you navigate your journey from banker to broker.

1. Always put the client first

Your clients are the backbone of your business, and focusing on their best interests is key to building trust and long-term success. This is different when you are a mortgage broker – you cannot limit yourself and only sell the products of the bank that employed you. You need to have at least a good understanding and awareness of the 60 lenders and thousands of loan products in the market.

There may be times when you have to take on deals that aren't immediately profitable at the start – like a client with a not-so-great credit score – but doing so demonstrates your commitment to the client's needs. This encourages word-of-mouth marketing, which remains the most powerful way to grow your clientele regardless of industry. Imagine a client comes to you with a deal that doesn't offer a big upfront commission. If you prioritise their long-term financial well-being, they're more likely to return to you for future deals and send referrals your way.

2. Lead by example

Great leaders inspire those around them. If you decide to work under an established broker, make sure your morals align. As a broker, you should embody your company's values in every interaction. Whether it's with their clients, the customer service team or referral partners, always act ethically, care about the people you work with and give back to your community. Give back without expecting anything in return. That is how you will add value and get people drawn towards you and want to become your clients. Down the line, they may choose to deal directly with you.

3. Support your team

Mortgage broking is no longer a solo game. You will need at least one other person if your business needs to operate on a day-to-day basis. Therefore, your success depends on your team's performance, and that's why fostering a healthy work–life balance is crucial.

You cannot demand that your team member(s) work harder than you; as Gary Vee says, 'It is your business, not theirs'. When your support staff feels valued and trusted, they're more motivated to go above and beyond. Instead of clockwatching, let your team take ownership of their work. Give them the flexibility to manage their time while ensuring high-quality results. This trust fosters loyalty and keeps your operations running smoothly.

Most of the successful brokers have support staff who have been with them for years, as they allow the team to share in their success and appreciate them publicly.

4. Cast a wide net

Given the economy and interest rates, not many clients are in a position to buy. Referral partners, such as real estate agents and accountants, can be powerful allies in sending potential clients your way.

Establishing and maintaining strong relationships with these professionals are critical to ensuring a steady flow of leads. You will need to spend time educating these clients, even though you don't see immediate returns, and don't forget to refer clients back to them. Leads are a major pain point for every business owner, and I have seen financial planners make the silly mistake of thinking that servicing clients is enough to keep leads coming. It is not enough just servicing clients; you need to reciprocate their gesture.

Don't just rely on a few partners; keep an Excel sheet of incoming and outgoing leads. Diversify your network by partnering with financial planners, property developers and even driving schools. This will give you access to different markets and client bases.

5. Be seen, stay relevant

Brand visibility is crucial in establishing a presence, attracting new clients and remaining in competition. Consistency in branding builds trust and recognition in your community. Whether it's through social media, community engagement or a well-designed shopfront, ensure that your brand stays top of mind.

You can leverage social media platforms like LinkedIn, TikTok and Instagram to share success stories, client testimonials and industry tips. This not only keeps you relevant but also attracts new clients. Use AI if you are short of creativity or time or are camera-shy. You can also engage your team members and do videos together so you are not awkward talking alone into a camera.

Remember, marketing costs may be tax-deductible, so don't shy away from this spend!

6. Learn from the best

Don't be shy about reaching out to successful brokers for mentorship. I used to think that top brokers may be arrogant. To my surprise, they all want to give back! I have seen top brokers allow other brokers to come spend a day in their brokerage and do a study tour.

Even if they can't dedicate large amounts of time to you, many top brokers are happy to offer advice, share their experiences or let you join their team and tap into their resources. This does not, however, replace the need for a mentor if you've been in the industry for less than two years.

Look for mentors who align with your values and business goals. Surrounding yourself with successful people can give you the tools to emulate their success. If you can't get in the same room as them, watch the podcasts they do with advisers, with brokers and coaches and at events your aggregator holds.

7. Choose the right aggregator

Your aggregator is more than just an **Approved Products List** (APL) provider. They play a crucial role in supporting your business growth through compliance, marketing, professional development/training and commission rates.

Be honest with yourself on what you need support with. If you choose a flat fee model and expect the work, it won't happen; you'll get caught in the vicious circle of jumping from aggregator to aggregator for value. Once you are honest and upfront, both you and your aggregator can set expectations from the start, and you can hold them accountable. You have to spend money to make money, so don't buy an economy ticket and then demand meals reserved for business class.

8. Goal setting

I was surprised that only around 1% of all seasoned mortgage brokers had a business plan – they all seemed to have worked for a mortgage broker, saw how lucrative it was and decided to go out on their own without a plan. Today, however, given that there are 19,000 brokers competing with you, you need to know your target audience and competitors and plan how you'll attract and retain those customers.

As you'll see in the following chapters, you need to invest in your business, so you need to project your finances and build a buffer for the months you make no money. It's important to set both financial and operational goals for your business. Many brokers focus solely on settlement numbers, but it's equally important to understand your financials; deals never settle exactly when you expect them to.

You don't need to do a 40-page business plan. To start with, break your goals into short-term and long-term milestones. If your goal is to increase settlements by 20%, consider what operational changes (e.g., hiring outsourced staff and increasing marketing spend) will be required to meet that target.

9. Overcome quiet times

The quieter periods in the market, like the holiday season, are a great opportunity to nurture relationships with past clients. A quick phone call (rather than a text) can make your clients feel appreciated. They may open up about a purchase they may be thinking of financing, and you could forward that lead to a trusted referral partner. For your own business, there's nothing like it if you are able to reprice the client and save them money when they are expecting to spend.

10. Team management

Running a smooth brokerage requires a strong operational process. Don't have it in your head and expect your team members to be mind-readers. Develop a blueprint for how your business operates – from lead generation to settlement – document it and go over it with your team members. If they come up with suggestions, don't ignore them – if it saves them time, they will do it their way, only leaving you disgruntled. It is better to agree with them from the onset. You need to ensure each member of your team knows exactly what their job entails. At the same time, don't do their job. It is hard to delegate and automate, but it has to be done. Don't forget to then do a post settlement list of tasks too. This is the clencher.

Conclusion

The mortgage broking industry offers limitless potential, but success requires more than just knowledge of financial products. By focusing on customer-centric strategies, building strong referral networks, maintaining effective team management and continuously learning and adapting, you'll set yourself up for sustained growth and profitability.

The key to thriving in this industry is resilience, adaptability and a commitment to providing excellent service. With these strategies in hand, you're ready to conquer the challenges of mortgage broking and build a business that stands the test of time!

CHAPTER 2

From PAYG to self-employed: Understanding the costs of becoming a mortgage broker

Making the leap from being a **pay as you go (PAYG)** employee to a self-employed mortgage broker is an exciting yet challenging transition. It promises flexibility, the potential for uncapped earnings and the freedom to craft your own path. But with that freedom comes huge responsibility and costs. Understanding the startup expenses and ongoing costs of running your own business is crucial for anyone considering this move. A lot of prospective bankers aren't aware of all the total costs, and that is one question always asked to recruiters at different aggregators.

In this chapter, we'll break down the key financial considerations when transitioning from a salaried professional to a self-employed mortgage broker. Whether you're a seasoned banker looking to go independent or someone new to the field, knowing where your money needs to go will set you up for success.

1. Education and licensing

To operate as a mortgage broker, you'll need the right qualifications and licensing. Mortgage broking has the lowest entry requirement in terms of education. The initial cost of your education and certification is relatively modest but essential. While the Certificate IV is the minimum qualification, brokers in Australia must complete a diploma in finance and mortgage broking management, which is usually a one-time cost that ensures you meet industry standards.

- **Education costs (Diploma): $1,300**

2. Structuring your business

When going self-employed, you'll need to decide on a business structure. Should you set up a sole trader, a company or a trust? Proper structuring can help optimise taxes and protect your assets, but it requires professional advice from an accountant or tax agent. Consulting an accountant and contracts lawyer early, and preferably at the start of the financial year, will help you determine the best way to set up your entity to ensure it aligns with your long-term goals.

- **Structuring (accounting and legal advice)**: **$4,000**

- **Establishment of a company**: **$3,000**

3. Aggregator fees

Joining an aggregator is essential for accessing **customer relationship management (CRM)** systems, getting accredited and building relationships with lenders. Aggregators also provide training, marketing support and business development services. Higher the level of support, higher the fees, obviously. These fees are approximate – most aggregators have fees in addition to tech fees and subscription fees, or offer options to bundle these fees – so make sure you get your head around the breakdown of these costs.

- **Aggregator fees (12 months)**: **$12,000**

4. Marketing and branding

First impressions matter, so getting your marketing and branding right early on can help you establish a strong foundation. To attract clients to you, you'll need to invest in a professional website, client meetings, gifts, events and other marketing activities. Your aggregator can help you with sourcing the right marketing professionals who could do everything – from old-school business cards to setting up a website and social media presence. You could also easily find one on freelance marketplace platforms such as Airtasker, Upwork and Fiverr.

Ensuring you have a digital presence is critical to compete in today's market. Even if you have no interest, employ the skills of those who understand this landscape – like someone skilled with search engine optimisation (SEO) to increase your visibility in search engine results and drive more traffic to your website or landing page.

- **Marketing, socials & website costs**: **$12,000**

5. Mentoring and networking

Starting out, you'll benefit from mentorship to guide you through the complexities of the industry. They have been through the ups and downs. They don't just provide advice but spend time to review your work and work on implementing the advice they give you.

Investing in networking is also crucial and non-negotiable. The more people you come across, the more the learnings. Attend industry events and get-togethers hosted by potential referral partners. Mortgage broking can be a lonely profession, and no one can understand your anxieties better than another broker who has gone through or is in the same position as you.

- **Mentoring (2 years)**: **$15,000**

- **Networking and travel**: **$6,000**

6. Office set-up

Whether you rent a dedicated office, rent a shared workspace alongside other businesses or set up a home office, having a professional environment is key to staying organised, maintaining a work–life balance and being productive.

For brokers just starting out, you might choose to operate from home to minimise overhead, but budgeting for future office needs will help as your business grows. Your team will grow, and you would want them to work alongside you. Alternatively, working in the same premises as accountants, real estate agents, financial planners and business consultants will provide you with referral opportunities. It will also benefit to own an office within a self-managed superfund. More on that later.

- **Office rent/coworking spaces: $60,000**

- **Office utilities and expenses: $12,000**

7. Technology and hardware

A good laptop or MacBook, mobile phone and reliable internet are non-negotiables for running a smooth mortgage broking business. Invest in the best equipment you can afford because these are the tools that will make your job easier, allow you to work anywhere and get back to your clients sooner.

- **Phone: $1,300**

- **Laptop and small hardware: $3,000**

- **Internet and phone credit: $6,000**

8. Insurance and protections

When you go self-employed, you'll need to mark your calendar to review your own personal insurances, like income protection and professional indemnity insurance, to protect your business and livelihood. The costs below are the average and will be higher if you have pre-existing medical conditions or get insurance later in life.

- **Trauma and income protection insurance**: **$5,000**

- **Professional Indemnity Insurance (PI)**: **$2,000**

9. Software subscriptions

Ask any broker and they will have at least five favourite apps – Quickli, monday.com, FileInvite, XERO and Canva, to name a few. To run a successful broking business, you'll need access to various software platforms to manage leads, analyse data and submit loans. The industry has gone paperless, and everyone is trying to automate every element of the role. It saves you time and reduces error. Don't try and cut costs here, as it is the way of the future.

- **Subscriptions**: **$6,000**

10. Miscellaneous Expenses

As you build your business, there will be unexpected costs such as client refunds or legal fees. Setting aside a fund for these expenses will ensure you're prepared for anything. Being affiliated with industry bodies like the Mortgage & Finance Association of Australia (MFAA) and the Australian Financial Complaints Authority (AFCA) is essential for staying compliant.

- **Client refunds & legal costs**: **$5,000**

- **Industry memberships (AFCA: $395; MFAA: $671)**: **$1,066**

Total Estimated Cost: $154,666

This is a stretched figure to help you understand the various costs involved in transitioning from PAYG employment to running your own mortgage broking business. By preparing for these expenses, you can make an informed decision and start your business on solid financial footing. Better to inflate the anticipated costs and be prepared rather than find yourself short.

Conclusion

While the upfront costs of becoming a self-employed mortgage broker may seem daunting, the freedom, potential earnings and personal satisfaction that come from running your own business make it all worthwhile. Careful planning and budgeting will help you navigate this transition smoothly and position you for long-term success.

When you're ready to take the plunge, just remember that the money you spend now is an investment in your future. The sky's the limit when it comes to the rewards.

CHAPTER 3

Commission vs. PAYG mortgage brokers: Finding the best model for your business

When running a mortgage broking business, one of the most important decisions is whether to build a team of brokers on a commission-only or a PAYG basis. Having a team ensures that you can take time off and your clients are still being looked after. If you decide to sell in the future, for whatever reason, not being a sole trader business will work in your favour. This is because you may choose to bring in brokers with varied experience (commercial and asset) that will make your brokerage a one-stop shop for all things finance.

Each model has its strengths, weaknesses, opportunities and threats. Choosing the right one can significantly impact your business's profitability, growth and overall stability. In this chapter, we'll break down the differences between these two models using a SWOT analysis to help you determine which one best suits your business goals and risk tolerance.

Commission-only model

Strengths
Financial Flexibility: One of the biggest advantages of the commission-only model is its cost efficiency. Brokers are only paid an upfront and trail commission split when they successfully settle a loan, reducing the financial burden on the business. This model eliminates the fixed costs of paying a salary and helps keep expenses low, especially when leads are slow.

According to a 2019 industry survey, brokerages in Australia spend an average of $60,000 to $130,000 annually on salaried (PAYG) brokers. Commission-only brokers, on the other hand, are only compensated when they close deals, which can result in significant cost-savings during quieter months.

Weaknesses

Lead Dependency: Commission-only brokers often have a client base and generate their own leads. This is tough for newcomers. Additionally, the cost of acquiring leads in Australia can range between $20 to $150, which places pressure on the brokerage to maintain a consistent pipeline of clients to feed the newbie broker.

Burnout and Turnover: Commission-only brokers often work long hours to close deals. Reason being, they are more vested in these clients. They cannot afford to have a low conversion rate, and the lack of a base pay safety net can lead to burnout, which, in turn, can result in high turnover.

Opportunities

Scaling and Growth: Without the burden of fixed salaries, the commission-only model allows brokerages to scale rapidly. You can hire new brokers with minimal financial risk, and if they don't perform, they can be let go without the complications of employment laws. This model is particularly appealing to new or growing brokerages that need flexibility in their workforce due to tight cash flow.

Threats

High Risk of Burnout: Commission-only brokers need to constantly hustle – generating leads, closing deals, doing the admin and maintaining relationships with existing clients. Brokers who get burned out or don't generate an income at a level they did before going self-employed may leave the industry altogether.

PAYG Model

Strengths
Ownership and Retention: PAYG brokers offer more stability. Brokers on salary tend to stay longer due to the safety net of a stable income, which can build a solid foundation for long-term client relationships.

PAYG brokers have the added security of benefits like sick leave, annual leave and superannuation, which help reduce turnover and ensure you have a steady team that is motivated to meet long-term goals. This saves you time, as you don't have to constantly onboard and train your new employees.

Weaknesses
Wage Costs and Performance Pressure: Unlike commission-only brokers, PAYG brokers come with a fixed salary cost. Even if a broker has a slow month, away on holidays and doesn't settle any deals, the business still incurs the cost of their salary. In addition, the head broker or customer service staff has to make

time to look after those clients while the broker is away, thus weighing on your resources.

For instance, a PAYG broker might need to annually settle at least 60 loans of $500,000 each just to cover a basic salary of $80,000. This creates pressure on the business to generate consistent revenue to meet payroll and overhead expenses.

Opportunities

Long-Term Stability: While the commission-only model is great for rapid growth, the PAYG model offers the chance to build a stable and experienced team over time. The clients know your team and don't have to call you directly each time on the littlest of queries. You can even outsource your back office to brokers needing support for a short time and create another revenue stream that way, covering their expenses.

Threats

Performance Risk: The business takes on more financial risk with PAYG brokers. Brokers may not be as driven as they would if they have skin in the game. They normally aim to meet targets and aren't chasing settlement numbers that are above and beyond their current targets. This may require you to incentivise them, which comes at more of a cost to you.

Conclusion

The decision between these two models boils down to the business owner's risk tolerance, growth goals and people skills.

The commission-only model is best for businesses looking for quick growth and flexibility without taking on too much financial risk. It's ideal for brokerages that are confident in their ability to generate consistent leads. PAYG model, on the other hand, is suitable for businesses that prioritise long-term stability and want to retain experienced brokers who are looking for job security and a steady income stream. This model can help build a reliable trail book for the head broker and foster stronger client relationships.

CHAPTER 4

From PAYG to self-employed mortgage broker: Navigating the transition with confidence

Ruby, a super successful broker of Asian heritage, was a top banker earning over $250,000 annually. She gave it all up to go into the business fulltime. She had been working in the banking sector for over a decade, and while she had built a stable career, something inside her started to stir. Ruby said she would regularly sit at her work desk, watching the clock tick closer to 8 pm. Her role offered a steady paycheck, but she longed for more control over her time, flexibility and the possibility of building something that was entirely her own.

One evening, she met me and our mutual friend Mark, who had successfully transitioned from being a banker into running his own mortgage brokerage. His enthusiasm for his newfound autonomy and unlimited earning potential sparked something in Ruby. He shared stories of the challenges he faced in those early days of no guaranteed income, managing his own taxes and the constant hustle to acquire leads, but he assured Ruby that it was all worth it.

'The key', he said, 'is to have a plan. Don't just jump. Make the transition strategically.'

Transitioning from a stable PAYG banking role to becoming a self-employed mortgage broker is a significant move. It offers the promise of greater flexibility, autonomy and unlimited earning potential, but it also comes with a series of challenges and responsibilities. As exciting as it sounds, it is crucial to plan this transition strategically over the course of six months to two years.

Mark and I went through the points below with Ruby, as we wanted to pass on to her what we learnt.

1. Income

As a PAYG employee, your income is consistently bolstered by bonuses, perks and company benefits.

In contrast, a self-employed mortgage broker faces irregular income. You'll need to plan for the financial strain that comes with a lack of immediate commissions for at least the first six to eight months.

Action:
Build a safety net by saving at least 6–12 months' worth of living expenses before transitioning. While you are employed, build relationships with your clients and add them on LinkedIn, Facebook or any other channel so that they can reach you even if you change phone numbers and email addresses.

2. Taxation

In PAYG employment, taxes are automatically deducted, leaving you little to worry about until tax time. As a sole trader, you are responsible for managing your tax obligations. This includes tracking business income, filing **business activity statements (BAS)** every quarter, keeping receipts of expenses and ensuring compliance with Goods and Services Tax (GST), if applicable.

Action:
Hire a proactive bookkeeper and accountant to assist with financial management and provide you with business advisory services. Stay disciplined and

don't rely on others to make sure your finances are in order, so set aside time each weekend to update your accounting records.

3. Superannuation

In a PAYG role, superannuation contributions are made by your employer. As a sole trader, you are responsible for making your own super contributions. Without regular contributions, you risk falling behind in retirement savings. Don't rely on your trail book to see you through your retirement; trail payments dry up within four years of inactivity.

Action:
Set up a **self-managed super fund (SMSF)** or ensure that regular contributions are made to your existing superannuation account. Consider the tax benefits and insurance coverage tied to superannuation accounts. Insurances within super are cheaper, and it is hard to get that level of cover without exclusions, so make sure you don't lose it.

4. Business costs

As a self-employed broker, you bear all business-related expenses. These costs include office rent, technology, subscriptions, onshore/offshore staff wages, marketing, utilities and unforeseen expenses that are crucial to the success of your brokerage.

Action:
Carefully budget for all business costs, and ensure that cash flow is stable enough to cover these expenses. Review expenses regularly to avoid overcommitting. Make sure you can get business loans if you do need one in the interim.

5. Compliance

Mortgage brokers in Australia must adhere to specific regulations, including the **best interests duty (BID)**. Keeping up with these evolving requirements can be time-consuming but is critical for compliance.

Action:
Partner with a knowledgeable mentor, and engage your aggregator's broker success manager or partnership manager to stay compliant. Make sure you're on top of all legal obligations, and don't leave any slips to chance. The earlier you address a mistake, the easier it will be for your aggregator or compliance manager to assist you.

6. Liability

Operating as a sole trader means you have unlimited liability. This means your personal assets could be at risk in the event of business debts or legal claims. Naive brokers start a business with their **Australian Business Number (ABN)** and don't give this any thought.

Action:
Consider setting up a company or family trust structure to limit personal liability. Consult your accountant and lawyer to ensure the right business structure is in place to protect your assets.

7. Work–life balance

Transitioning to self-employment may require extended working hours, especially when building a client base. Managing clients' expectations and ensuring prompt responses can quickly blur the line between work and personal life. If you don't intend to work weekends, be upfront to avoid fallouts with your clients who may be driven by their feelings and instincts.

Action:
Set clear boundaries, but be prepared to be available when clients need you (especially on weekends when they go for house inspections).

8. Continuous professional development

As a self-employed broker, the onus is on you to make time to stay current with industry changes, lender policies and professional development. Even if it means spending three hours on the weekend, you have to maintain that discipline. Mastering digital tools and improving leadership, networking and communication skills are critical for business growth; it is no longer only about closing deals.

Action:
Commit to ongoing education. To ensure you're growing alongside your business, invest in sales training and leadership development or leverage free resources like LinkedIn Learning, aggregator-led courses and mentorship programs.

9. Client acquisition

Client acquisition is the cornerstone of a successful mortgage broking business. Building relationships and a reliable client base takes years, effort and constant communication. It is easier to buy profits than to make profits. This is the sure shot way to accelerate your growth and free you from working in your business 24/7 rather than on it. More on this later.

Action:

Network extensively with mature brokers and diversify your lead generation efforts. Express your willingness to buy trail books, and be vocal about how good your services are. Be open to working with all types of clients, and nurture your referral networks. Ensure you are prepared to manage offshore teams if required for client servicing.

10. Managing cash flow

Mortgage brokers are most vulnerable to economic shifts, changes in interest rates and property market downturns, which can directly impact your cash flow. Banks have special rates to pass to their clients, but brokers don't have that privilege.

Action:

Focus on building trail income for passive revenue, and maintain a healthy pipeline of upfront commissions that exceed your trail commissions month on month. Keep marketing and referral efforts active to stay ahead of slow periods.

11. Health

As a PAYG employee, you benefit from sick leave, annual leave and health insurance. These are luxuries that disappear when you go solo.

Health setbacks can have a significant impact on your business. If it is a prolonged illness, it could mean the end of your business for good. Keep your mind and body healthy. You don't have to become an athlete, but make sure you don't work yourself to the ground either.

Family is everything – there's no point if you become the most successful mortgage broker with no close family to enjoy your success with.

Action:
Keep default insurances active within your superfund, and secure trauma and income protection insurance. These policies can provide financial support in the event of illness or injury.

Conclusion

Transitioning from a PAYG banking role to a self-employed mortgage broker is an exciting but challenging journey. By planning for the financial, legal and professional hurdles ahead, you can set yourself up for success. Make sure you take time to reflect, prepare and build a solid, disciplined foundation before making the leap into the world of self-employment.

CHAPTER 5

Creating your value proposition: The key to standing out as a mortgage broker

In a highly competitive mortgage broking industry, understanding and clearly defining your value proposition can make or break your success. Surprisingly, many brokers don't recognise the importance of having a **unique value proposition (UVP)**, let alone understand how to craft one.

A value proposition goes far beyond just helping clients find a loan; it is a clear and compelling statement that explains how your services solve a customer's problem or improve their situation. It gives the ideal customer a reason to choose you over the competition by highlighting the unique benefits they'll receive from working with you. Say, with 19,000 brokers one could access, why would they come to you? Your UVP should offer a tailored financial solution that caters to each client's needs and ensures they feel supported and informed throughout their home-buying journey.

Why is a UVP important?

- It distinguishes your brand from others in the market.
- It focuses marketing efforts to attract the right audience.
- It increases customer engagement, setting expectations early.
- It guides your business strategy by clarifying your goals.
- It boosts sales conversions, as it communicates why clients should choose you.
- It builds trust and long-term relationships, leading to repeat business and referrals.

Here's a step-by-step approach for mortgage brokers to craft a strong value proposition:

1. Provide local insights

Clients expect their broker to know the local market inside and out, but adding national insight can take it a step further. Commence a newsletter and post on your socials providing regular, digestible updates on property prices, changes in lending criteria and economic trends that impact your clients' borrowing power. Offer market analysis reports from respected economists and help clients understand how changing interest rates or housing trends could affect their mortgage decisions. Don't just copy–paste, but try to make it palatable to your consumer in layman's terms.

Added value:
Clients appreciate brokers who go beyond numbers to offer practical insights into how economic factors affect their choices.

2. Custom mortgage solutions

Brokers must invest time in understanding each client's unique financial situation and long-term goals. This allows you to present personalised mortgage options from fixed-rate, variable loans, hybrid rates, interest-only and investment loans.

Customising solutions ensures the client gets a mortgage that suits their current circumstances but also has flexibility for future changes.

Added value:

Tailoring mortgage products shows clients that you're focused on finding the best solution for them to enter the property market sooner. It builds trust, as they know you have the tools to help them afford the loan going forward.

3. Approved panel of lenders (APL)

Let go of old habits of sticking with your favourite three or five lenders. Venture out to get to know different lenders. Diversify your offerings by working with a wide range of lenders, including major banks, credit unions and non-bank lenders.

This diversity ensures you don't get caught up with any compliance issues. Have options for all types of clients – even those with less-than-ideal credit histories, self-employed, new to the country on visas or those operating newer businesses (like those with ABNs less than two years old).

Added value:

Being able to access multiple lenders increases the likelihood of securing better deals for clients, which makes your service invaluable.

4. Digital application

Leverage technology to streamline the loan application and approval process. From online application tools to e-signatures, implementing tech will not only save time but also keep clients updated in real time.

It is easier for you to have the documents readily accessible, should any issues arise. Many clients come back asking you to send them a copy later on, and scanning documents is not productive. If files are online, you save space in your office and can get to files quicker. It can be exhausting learning new tech, but the dollar and manual effort it saves are totally worth it.

Added value:

Efficiency, speed and transparency through digital tools will impress clients and reduce friction in their journey.

5. Proactive negotiations

Use your relationships with lenders to negotiate better terms. The topmost brokers get their way with banks through their connections with **business development managers (BDMs)** and state directors – whether that's securing lower interest rates, waiving fees or adjusting repayment structures to suit your client's needs.

Don't cancel the meetings with your BDMs. Sometimes you may feel the coffee catch-up is not required, but if you help the BDM meet their catch-up targets, chances are they will want to have your back too. Regularly review your clients' mortgages and mark your calendar for loan anniversaries – make sure you call and not take the easy way out by sending a text.

Added value:
Proactive care for existing clients through renegotiation and refinancing creates lasting relationships.

6. Honest communication

One of the most critical parts of any business relationship is honest communication. Be upfront about what's possible and what isn't. Setting clear expectations from the start, regarding your services, fees and potential limitations, saves both you and the client time and frustration. I know of a broker who would make the client sign the engagement letter, even if they weren't 100% confident that the lenders would allow the servicing.

Added value:
Transparency builds trust. Clients will appreciate your honesty and later avoid complaining and hounding you constantly.

7. Best practices

Maintaining strict compliance with the **best interests duty (BID)** is essential. Keep your industry knowledge up to date by regularly participating in training through your aggregator. It could be boring and many brokers don't show up for these sessions, but you don't know what you could be missing out on. This not only ensures you're always offering the best possible advice but also keeps your business safe from legal or regulatory pitfalls.

Added value:
Adhering to best practices and industry standards ensures clients receive ethical and top-tier service that protects your livelihood.

8. Referral network

Encourage referrals by offering client testimonials and creating a rewards program for successful referrals. Partnering with real estate agents, financial planners and accountants can create a steady flow of clients. I know it is easy to say and it's not easy working with them, but business is all about networking. No longer can you put your head down and get on with work. Collaboration and community are key.

Added Value:
Building a referral program strengthens your network and opens doors for future business.

9. Client education

Position yourself as a thought leader by hosting seminars and webinars for potential clients. Offer to speak when your referral partners organise events. For example, educating first-home buyers about grants and financing options not only builds credibility but also ensures clients are well-informed. It shows the clients that a team – a stupendous real estate agent and you – is working for them, to see them get their foot in the door.

Added value:

Clients who feel educated and empowered by their broker are more likely to refer you to others. They could forward and tag your posts on social media, extending your reach without additional marketing investment from you.

10. Personalised service

According to an article about a mortgage broker sales process by BrokerEngine, the first broker to respond to a client's inquiry is often the one who gets the business. The quickest broker gets back to the query in 90 minutes. Top brokers have testified that this is key to their success.

Responding quickly and offering customised communication keeps you front of mind. Personalise your service to cater to individual clients' communication preferences. Pay heed whether they are comfortable with Zoom, face-to-face meetings or phone calls, and don't call them when they've requested an email. They could be at work, unable to take the call and have a private discussion with you.

Added value:

Fast responses and personalised service will help differentiate you from brokers who take a one-size-fits-all approach.

Conclusion

In today's competitive market, mortgage brokers who take the time to craft a clear and compelling value proposition will not only attract more clients but also build deeper and longer-lasting relationships. Focus on the points above and think about what makes your service unique – is it your industry expertise, customer service or network of lenders?

Recap of Section 1: Understanding the basics of mortgage broking

Chapter 1: Building trust and relationships

- Build a strong referral network (beyond real estate agents and financial planners).

- Maintain active visibility on platforms like LinkedIn and Instagram. Create valuable content and share client success stories.

Chapter 2: Transitioning from PAYG to self-employed

- Plan for all startup costs like education, business structuring, marketing, office space and tech.

- Save 6 to 12 months of living expenses to prepare.

- Set up your business structure early (sole trader, company or trust).

- Engage a proactive accountant for tax and budgeting.

Chapter 3: Choosing the right business model (commission vs. PAYG brokers)

- Decide between commission-only brokers (low cost but can lead to burnout) or PAYG brokers (stable but higher costs).

- If scaling quickly, commission-only is flexible.

- If building long-term stability, PAYG allows for a stronger team foundation.

- Every six months, match your model to your business goals.

Chapter 4: Navigating the PAYG to self-employed transition

- Build a client base while still employed. Connect with clients on LinkedIn and save their contact info.

- Save a financial buffer for irregular income.

- Hire a bookkeeper and keep detailed records of expenses and tax obligations on XERO.

- Set boundaries for work–life balance, but be available when clients need you, especially on weekends.

Chapter 5: Creating a unique value proposition

- Clearly define why clients should choose you over others.

- Leverage technology for a smoother loan process (e-signatures, Quickli and online applications).

- Proactively negotiate better terms for clients by building strong relationships with lenders and always staying honest and transparent in your communication.

CHAPTER 6

Boosting the value of your trail book

A trail book is a list of clients with recurring revenue from commissions on active loans that brokers receive based on the life on the loan. It offers brokers something to fall back on. Most brokers see this as an enticing reason to go out on their own rather than solely rely on the upfront commission split they receive if they work under a head broker or bank.

A few years ago, it was scrutinised during the Royal Commission as it raised concerns whether this trail commission offered value to clients even though brokers weren't actively servicing clients. This led to discussions on whether they should be banned or restructured. The government decided to retain trail commissions with stronger emphasis on compliance, retention and ongoing support.

Your trail book is the heart and soul of your mortgage business. Your pride and joy. It's not just valuable to you but also a major asset to your aggregator, so when the time comes to sell, you don't want to rush. A hasty sale can leave you with far less than what your trail book is truly worth.

Why are we talking about selling already? Always start with the end in mind. It is not just retirement that could take you out. It could be health, burnout or choosing a new career path.

Let's break down how you can prep your trail book for maximum value in a way that's easy to follow and keeps things simple. It is lucid so that it can make sense to someone new to the mortgage broking.

Give yourself time

Think of your trail book as a tree. It takes time. You plant the seed and nurture it so it can grow and produce fruit over time. Ideally, you should prepare for a sale over a period of three months to five years. Yes, it's a wide range but that's because bigger books take more time to get right and attract buyers.

The bigger and healthier your book and the less risky it seems to buyers, the more confident they'll be in paying a good price for it. Use this time to not just grow the numbers but also get to know your clients better. Understanding who they are and what made them stay with you makes your book even more valuable.

Data is your secret weapon

We live in a world overflowing with data, and it's your best friend when it comes to increasing your trail book's value. At first when you start using a CRM, you get annoyed by all the fields you need to fill, all the information in the application. Why do you need to rekey them in the database? It is for good reason. Later, you can spit out a report to spot trends and build a case on how organised you are. The incoming broker can come in and take off from exactly the point you stopped. Tracking key details, besides just the loan details, will help you understand the strengths and weaknesses of your business.

Asking these questions can help you start:

- How many leads did I generate this month?
- How many clients are coming off fixed-rate loans?
- What's the average loan size this year compared to last year?

- How long does it take me to close deals and what's causing any delays?

These are the pressing questions that need to be answered right away. They help you keep track of your business in a way that buyers can easily understand and trust.

Use your CRM

If tracking data feels overwhelming, don't worry. You're not alone. Most aggregators provide **customer relationship management (CRM)** tools and outsourcing support who can look after the data entry. The key is to make it a habit right from the start.

Even when you're swamped, try to put an hour at the end of the day in the diary to input data regularly. If you miss a few days, that's okay. Set a weekly reminder to update your numbers. Don't let it go for too long, as that is when procrastination sets in. As you see the numbers grow and see patterns on what's working age-wise, income-wise and location-wise, you'll feel more focused and motivated to stay on top of things. Think of it like checking your Instagram or TikTok likes – once you start, it becomes addictive in the best way possible.

Key numbers to track

To make things even easier, here's a simple checklist to get you started:

- New loans vs. refinanced loans
- Fixed, variable and hybrid loans
- Principal and interest vs. Interest-only loans
- First home buyers vs. investment property buyers
- Clients under 45 vs. over 45
- Top 10 clients by value
- Residential loans vs. asset finance loans
- Top 3 lenders
- Top 3 referral partners

Start small and build on these. If you're not sure where to get this info, ask your aggregator's business development manager (BDM). They're there to help and can provide you with a business insights report (a document that pulls all this data together). They pull reports weekly and monthly to track their own business performance – and your business performance affects their business performance.

Know your worth

When the time comes to sell, all the data you've collected will give you the power to confidently name your price. You won't just be guessing or quoting three times because that is what you heard Joe sold it for. You'll have proof to back up your asking price.

The more transparent your business, the more appealing it is to sellers. A commission report with redacted last names or loan numbers doesn't tell them anything. Who are those clients? What type of service do they expect? Are they at an age where they may downsize or pay the whole loan off? Do they have kids who may want to buy? Imagine how you would feel if you saw a trail book where more than 70% of the clients were self-employed. I bet the thought got you salivating. The more the opportunities are coming in, the more willing buyers will be to open their wallets.

Conclusion

By focusing on growth, tracking data and understanding the value of your business right from the start, you'll set yourself up for success and create a trail book that's irresistible to buyers.

CHAPTER 7

Getting the right price: Understanding the valuation multiple for your trail book

Scott had been in the mortgage broking business for over 25 years. He had worked tirelessly over the years and had been a huge part of the BNI community, nurturing client relationships and keeping up with the ever-changing regulations. He had built a steady stream of income from his trail book and knew it was time to start planning his exit. With an eye on retirement, Scott began thinking about selling his trail book.

One evening, over dinner at an aggregator conference, Scott met Jeff, an old colleague who had sold his trail book just a few years earlier. The conversation shifted towards the process of selling. Jeff had sold the rights to his trail commission to an investment company, but the deal had been far more complex than Scott anticipated.

'It's not just about selling the book,' Jeff warned, 'There's the client base, referral payments and potential liabilities. You need to know exactly what you're selling and who you're selling it to.'

That conversation opened Scott's eyes. He realised there were many nuances to selling a trail book that went beyond the numbers. There were buyers out there who wanted the trail but weren't interested in the clients. Others would make him sign guarantees about maintaining the trail for years to come. It was clear that selling a trail book was more than just cashing out; it was about protecting the value of everything he'd built. That is when Scott reached out to our team to understand his options.

Getting the right valuation for your trail book is key to making sure you walk away with what it's worth.

What's a valuation multiple?

The value of your trail book is usually expressed as a multiple of the current trail revenue. Essentially, it's a way of multiplying your recurring revenue to get a selling price. So, how do these multiples work?

The lowest multiple I've seen is 2x – meaning a buyer will pay two times the current trail revenue. The highest is 3.7x, which is often offered to brokers with large, well-balanced books and a solid reputation in the industry.

If you're caught up in compliance issues or urgently need cash, your multiple will likely be on the lower end (around 2x). On the flip side, if your trail book is robust and diversified and you've built a great name in the industry, expect something closer to 3x.

Why multiples vary

There's no one-size-fits-all multiple. A lot of brokers mistakenly believe they should get the same multiple no matter what. Not true. Your multiple depends on where your business stands in its lifecycle: Startup, Growth, Maturity or Decline.

If you think you deserve the highest multiple, go back and revisit your numbers. This chapter provides valuable guidance, and work with a proactive accountant to help you fill any value gaps and get the best deal.

Why trail books are so attractive

Here's why brokers are lining up to buy trail books: They generate predictable and passive income, for the time being at least. If you look after the clients, you will earn your money back sooner. Compare it to a high-interest savings account, which might earn you around 5.55% per year. A trail book, on the other hand, can generate 0.15% trail commission – and that adds up quickly over time! Buyers aren't just purchasing a book, they're buying a steady income stream and an opportunity to grow their own existing business.

Buyers need data to perform their due diligence. They're investing money in exchange for a well-predictable long-term income. And let's face it – that's a pretty sweet deal when done right.

What to watch out for

When selling your trail book, remember that it's not covered by your professional indemnity (PI) insurance going forward. That's important because it adds an extra layer of risk, so make sure you've considered all the details before moving forward. Call your PI insurance provider and get the expiry and enquire on how to put your PI in runoff.

Also, if you manage more than one trail book, keep an eye on the revenue you're receiving from each of those trail books. Fees can chip away at your income, and some aggregators will stop paying trail commissions if the amount falls below a certain threshold. If your book shrinks too much, you may find it difficult or impossible to sell.

Growing beyond $20,000 a month

If your trail book brings in over $20,000 a month, it might be time to get extra hands on deck to help you with retention. Why? The word on the street is that a trail book can lose around 25% of its value over four to five years due to attrition. However, with the potential end of clawbacks in sight, this number may shrink. Keeping clients happy and sticking with you will be the key to maintaining your trail book's value.

Conclusion

In the end, selling your trail book is all about preparation and timing. Whether you're aiming for a 2x or 3x multiple, remember that your book's value is directly tied to how well you know it, manage it and prepare it for sale. So, dig in to the data, collaborate with a business broker and position yourself for the best deal possible. After all, your trail book is your legacy. Make sure you get what it's worth!

CHAPTER 8

The strategic advantage: Why buying a trail book is a smart move for brokers

Mortgage broking is a service business. Realistically, you can only do two to three deals a week comfortably – and that's when you are relatively experienced. With this, imagine the rate at which you grow. It is often said, 'It's easier to buy profits than to make them.' For brokers who want to grow their business quickly, buying a trail book can be a game-changer.

With advancements in technology, the benefits of acquiring trail books are now available to brokers everywhere, whether they're in major cities or regional areas. The younger, savvy generation is the type who want to see their broker face to face in an office. Thanks to COVID and online meeting channels, they are happy to see you online, giving you the benefit to cast your net wider than your local postcode.

That doesn't mean you can just call your aggregator and they will provide you with a trail book that is available. There is a food chain, a hierarchy competition there. Brokers who write bigger volumes and have a stronger relationship with their BDMs have access to these opportunities before you. But don't sit and wait for your turn – speak to as many brokers as you can, regardless of age. It is not just a senior age broker who will sell. Many brokers lack the tenacity and are ready to throw in the towel if you name their price, so don't keep this intention of buying a trail book private. Mention it at every broker meeting opportunity.

Let's dive into why buying a trail book can be one of the smartest moves you'll make.

1. Passive revenue stream

One of the biggest advantages of buying a trail book is the immediate access to consistent passive income. As we hear brokers say, 'It's quiet at the moment' with property prices rising and loan demand slowing, a healthy trail book ensures that your business doesn't come to a halt during slow months. Even when upfront commissions dry up, your trail income keeps flowing for a bit, helping cover operational costs like staff salaries, subscriptions and other operational costs.

For instance, some brokers mention that when they contact clients for a check-in, the clients ask for loan top-ups. Sure, it's not always the work you're hoping for, but more loan balances mean more trail commissions. Over time, this compounds into a steady income that can help you invest in growing your business.

A steady trail revenue also allows you to reinvest in your business, whether that's hiring more onshore staff or upgrading your tech stack. Smart businesses, regardless of industry, are always looking for ways to improve cash flow, and having a trail book provides the safety net you need when the market shifts unexpectedly.

2. Instant client base

Buying a trail book gives you instant access to an existing client base. This means no more grinding away to build your list one client at a time. It's like being handed the keys to a fully functioning business with a loyal clientele. In mergers and acquisitions, size matters. Bigger businesses with more robust trail books tend to have lower risk due to its diversified client base, which attracts potential partners, investors and buyers down the line.

If your trail book generates over $500,000 annually, you can expect a higher valuation multiple, increasing the book's attractiveness. Many brokers mistakenly believe that it's harder to sell a big trail book, but aggregators are often well-connected with buyers who can make large purchases.

A large trail book reflects a business that has established systems, processes and client management practices that can be replicated to support future growth. Most top brokers are looking for big trail books rather than small ones. This increased cash flow gives the buyer the power to expand their business even further, whether through acquisitions or by investing in marketing or additional services. It has a flow on effect.

3. Cross-selling

In an unpredictable market, where rates are fluctuating and the Reserve Bank hasn't made any changes for months, diversification is key. When you buy a trail book, you gain access to clients who may need more than just home loans. This opens doors for cross-selling other financial products such as:

- asset finance
- commercial loans
- business loans
- home and contents insurance
- utility bill reviews.

Brokers can also tap in to the referral power of their new clients. If you keep in touch and provide excellent service, your clients may refer new prospects to you, which helps you grow your network organically.

Some brokers worry they'll need to learn new loan types, like commercial or asset finance, but thanks to modern aggregator systems you can simply refer clients within your aggregator's network and earn referral income without needing to handle the process yourself. I get it, there is only so much brain power a broker business owner has.

4. Succession planning

If you're considering retirement in the next five to ten years or you're simply feeling burnt out, buying a trail book can be a succession strategy. It acts as a form of insurance if things don't go to plan, whether due to sickness, injury or disability. It also provides your successor (or key staff) a headstart with an already established client base.

A trail book is more than just numbers. It represents years of hard work and relationship-building. Having a tangible asset like a trail book means your business isn't just a legacy, it's something with real monetary value. Unlike asset finance brokers, mortgage brokers can lean on their trail books as they wind down their businesses.

Conclusion

Acquiring a trail book isn't just a quick transaction. It's a strategic decision with long-term benefits. From boosting your revenue to solidifying your brand and expanding your client base, the advantages are endless. But remember, just holding onto a trail book won't work. You need to work on the book, whether that means setting aside time to service your clients or hiring staff to manage it for you. A 'set and forget' approach won't yield the results you want.

Make your trail book investment count. Whether you're growing your business, preparing for succession or simply securing a more stable income, buying a trail book is a move that can help you thrive.

CHAPTER 9

Cracking the code: Common and uncommon ways to value your trail book

Valuing a trail book is like putting a price tag on your years of hard work, relationships and recurring income. Whether you're planning to retire or simply shift gears in your business, it's crucial to know the worth of your trail book.

Many brokers think they can just ask around for the going rate and use a one-size-fits-all method, but that's far from reality. Then, there are those brokers who are led by their heart, not their head. They think they can quote ten times the price, as they have put all their blood, sweat and tears in the business. It doesn't work like that.

Value is based on tangibles. The buyers aren't repaying you for the time you've invested but for the opportunities your efforts have created going forward.

Every trail book is different, and understanding how to properly value it is key to getting a fair deal. Ask any business broker or seasoned trail book buyer, they will tell you the art and the science that goes behind them buying a trail book. The brokers who are relationship-centric go by gut, while the analytical and strategic crunch the numbers and have different formulas they apply. It is not a bet that they put down. They know what they are looking for and the return they need to generate on their investment. Ideally, they wish to recoup what they've invested in two to four years.

Let's dive into some common and not-so-common methods to value your trail book.

1. Multiple of trail income: The industry favourite

This is the go-to method for most brokers, and it's the simplest. Basically, you take the annual trail commission and multiply it by a set factor, usually between 2x and 3x.

The multiple depends on the quality of your book. If your data is well-organised and your clients are loyal, you're looking at the higher end of the spectrum.

For instance, if your trail book generates $100,000 annually in trail commissions and the multiple is 3x, the value of your book would be $300,000.

Right now, a common scenario is:

- **2x** for basic trail books with minimal client engagement or poor data.

- **3x** for trail books with clean data and strong client relationships.

2. Discounted cash flow (DCF): The less used but powerful option

The DCF method is more about forecasting future cash flow. How much trail commission will you make in the years to come? But here's the catch: Not all dollars are created equal. Money today is worth more than the same amount in the future (because of inflation, investment opportunities, etc.). This method also takes into account the risks like clients paying off their loans early or switching brokers.

To sum it up: DCF calculates the present value of future income. The discount rate you use here is key, and less than 10% of brokers opt for this method.

3. Net present value (NPV) of future profits: The rarely used profit-centric approach

This is a bit similar to DCF, but with a twist – it looks at profits, not just revenue. You take into account how much it costs to maintain the trail book. Think of it as calculating how much you're actually left with after expenses.

It's not a method you'll see often, but it can be useful for businesses that are heavily focused on cost management.

4. Comparative analysis: The apples-to-apples approach

If you're into benchmarking, this is for you. Comparative analysis means looking at other recent trail book sales and using them as a yardstick. But be careful – you need to compare books that are similar in terms of client quality, broker reputation, client age and book diversification. It's not as simple as saying, 'That broker got x amount for their book, so I should too.' There's nuance involved.

Ask yourself: What's your business's unique value proposition? A broker brand that stands out with strong client engagement or niche expertise will fetch more. If you want to stand out, your trail book has to have something special, and that should be reflected in the valuation.

Conclusion

Valuing a trail book isn't all about plugging numbers into a formula. Sure, it's about understanding your business, your clients and your potential for growth too, and yes, data matters, but so do relationships, client retention and the potential for future earnings. If you're buying or selling, multiple face-to-face meetings are a great idea. They help build rapport, ensure cultural fit and give you a clearer picture beyond the spreadsheets.

Understanding the ins and outs of these valuation methods means you can approach the sale (or purchase) of your trail book with confidence, knowing you're getting a fair deal that reflects the true value of your business.

CHAPTER 10

Buying a trail book: A simple guide for new brokers

If you're a banker and have never purchased a trail book before, you might be wondering what's the deal with trail books and why they are so valuable. Many brokers think they aren't ready to buy. They think the only way to get their hands on a trail book is cold, hard cash.

That is not true.

One way is working under a head broker and building your trail book under them. The head broker will take the bigger cut of the commissions you generate, and you get the smaller cut. Likely splits are 60/40 or 70/40 of the trail commissions. Then, when you are ready, you can buy your trail book from the head broker. You pay them for the value you have created and ensure the head broker profits from the sale.

The other way is to work with a real estate agent or guarantor who wants to get into a **joint venture (JV)** with you. They provide the upfront capital to buy the trail. The agent/guarantor will take a share of that income stream, depending on the terms of the JV. You may eventually either buy out their share over time, or they continue to share profits from the trail book indefinitely until you negotiate a full buyout.

During a recent chat with an up-and-coming broker in Western Australia earlier this year, they mentioned how they only just realised the true value of their trail book and how it's an ongoing revenue stream for their business. This inspired me to break down the basics for all the brokers out there who might be new to the industry or unfamiliar with how hot trail book sales are.

What exactly is a trail book?

Think of a trail book as your client database. It's a list of clients you've built over the years, and each one generates recurring revenue in the form of trail commissions. These commissions are paid by lenders for the life of the loan, giving you a steady income stream. One of the easiest ways to track your trail book is through the commission statements your aggregator provides with each pay cycle.

Trail books are valuable because they represent passive income (the holy grail for any broker); once you've built a good list of clients, you don't always have to chase new business. You can rely on the steady revenue that comes in from your existing clients. However, you need to keep in touch with them and maintain a relationship to keep that income flowing.

Why would a broker sell their trail book?

You might wonder, 'Why would anyone sell this golden goose?'. There are a few reasons brokers choose to sell:

- Retirement or leaving the industry.
- Immediate cash needs.
- Focusing on other parts of their business.
- Personal reasons, like health or a lifestyle change.

A top broker in Victoria we spoke with couldn't understand why anyone would sell their trail book. His exit strategy is simple. He's holding on to his book until the day he dies. He even showed us proof of how his trail income stayed consistent, while other brokers complained about clawbacks and other losses. His strategy? Keep growing and maintaining your book for at least three to five years before you even think about selling.

How is a trail book valued?

Valuing a trail book isn't as simple as multiplying your annual trail commission. It involves diving into financial and non-financial data. Buyers look at things like:

Client quality: Younger and financially stable clients are more valuable because they'll have financial needs for a longer time.

Client retention: A high retention rate is gold. But remember, things like clawbacks, discharges and clients paying off loans early can chip away at the value.

Age of the book: Older books may have established relationships, but they can also have outdated client information and less diversification. Whereas, newer books may show better client engagement.

Diversification: A well-diversified trail book (clients, lenders and referral sources) is less risky for buyers. It won't be as affected by policy changes or demographic shifts.

Tips for brokers looking to buy a trail book

For brokers wanting to jump start their business, buying a trail book can be a fantastic investment. But, here are a few things to keep in mind:

Due diligence is key. Don't rush in. Study the client list, review the revenue stream and make sure the trail commissions are consistent. If you're not sure what to look for, reach out to your aggregator's mergers and acquisitions (M&A) team or your BDM for guidance. If they cannot help, seek a business broker who works exclusively with mortgage brokers.

Relationships matter. After you buy a trail book, it's all about relationships. Start building rapport with existing clients right away. Communicate twice – once when you take over the book, and again in six months to reinforce the connection. Overcommunication is better than flying under the radar here.

Get expert advice. Talk to your accountant to make sure buying the trail book doesn't mess up any tax planning or budgeting you've already done, and consult industry experts who know the mortgage broking world. Brokers tend to go out to forums and ask the whole wide world before starting with their aggregator, who is charging them fees to provide this kind of support – but if you don't know where to start, ask your aggregator.

Negotiate fairly: Don't just aim to get the lowest price; make sure the deal is fair for both sides. If you try to undercut the seller, you could lose goodwill and end up with a rocky post-sale transition. Put yourself in their shoes and negotiate with empathy. You may need the seller to come in at some point, and if you ripped them off, they will ignore you when you need them.

Conclusion

Buying a trail book is an excellent way to build or expand your business, especially if you're looking for consistent revenue. By following the basics and doing your homework, you can get one of the best returns on investment available in today's market.

Knowledge is power. Remember, the more you understand your trail book, the better deal you'll get, regardless of whether you're buying or selling.

CHAPTER 11

Mastering the art of selling your trail book: Get the best price

Your trail book is like your baby. You nurtured and grew it over the years. It's a steady stream of income that provides security, so when it comes time to sell, it's not just about dollars and cents.

You need to be able to articulate why buyers should not miss out on the opportunity to buy your book. While most brokers are experiencing inconsistent trail payments, what keeps your trail consistent? Who are those clients who have a solid history with you? What have you done to not let them wander off? What untapped potential for additional services is there in your book? If staying on to assist client handover will give you a better price, would you agree to stay on or would you get less but gain the ability to walk away from it completely?

It's about letting go of something personal. But, let's make one thing clear: The price you get for your trail book is not about luck. There's a strategy to getting the best price, and it's a mix of knowing your worth, understanding the buyer's perspective and playing your cards right.

Let's break it down.

1. What is the trail worth?

First things first, you need to understand what your trail book is truly worth. Every trail book is different, and thinking yours is worth the same as another broker's down the street could be a big mistake. Some things to consider are the:

- annual trail commission (inclusive of fees, charges and GST)
- diversity of loans (a good mix of loan types is more attractive)
- age of loans and future opportunities (past the clawback period)
- strength of client relationships (adds credibility and value).

Getting a professional valuation of your trail book is a smart move. Think of it like getting a trail book colonoscopy – a deep dive into your book's metrics, which can reveal some hard-to-digest insights. And trust me, this knowledge will be a game-changer when it comes to negotiation.

2. The buyer's perspective

Not all buyers are looking for the same thing. Some brokers will value the client relationships you've built, while others might just focus on the dollars – the trail income itself. By understanding what your buyer cares about, you can tailor your negotiation approach to highlight those aspects of your trail book.

3. Realistic asking price

A common mistake is setting an asking price that's too high, thinking your book is worth 10x the annual trail commission when it's not. You'll scare buyers away, or they'll deem you crazy and won't engage.

Use your professional valuation as a guide, and look at recent trail book sales in your area to gauge the right price. This will keep your expectations grounded and keep the buyers still wanting to go for it.

4. Justify your price

Buyers will **always** try to haggle; it's just part of human nature. So, be prepared to back up your price with data – the strength of your client base, the diversity of your loans and the future earning potential of your book.

If you plan to completely get out of the industry, that takes off the risk even more and you can get more for your book. If you decide you still want to stay in broking but work for someone else, in spite of a non-compete clause, the brokers will not want to pay top dollar for the book. After all, how much do NDAs and non-compete clauses hold up? No broker has the time to chase after you if you do break the terms of non-engaging with your existing clients for whatever reason.

5. Flexibility on terms

While sticking to your asking price is important, being flexible with terms can keep the negotiations flowing. For example:

- Would you like to stay on and work in the business after the sale?

- Would you send future referrals to the buyer?

- Do you want all the money upfront, or are you open to staggered payments?

- Are you okay with your staff transitioning to work for the buyer?

These questions can help you figure out where you're willing to compromise, making the deal more attractive to both parties. Don't be afraid to change your mind till you sign on the dotted line, especially if a clause works in your favour.

Ask your mentor and business broker for advice, and don't randomly seek advice from people if they don't know you or your business.

6. Cultivate multiple interested buyers

Nothing boosts your negotiating power like having multiple buyers at the table. Not only does this validate the value of your trail book, but it also puts you in a position to leverage competing offers. If a buyer knows there's competition, they're more likely to put forward their best offer quickly.

Don't limit yourself to just one broker, reach out to your aggregator's network to cast a wider net.

In the last round, narrow down the buyers to the top five. Do an informal Excel table where you work out the pros and cons.

Don't stop responding to the other buyers till you have sealed the deal. Deals often fall through, and you don't want to burn bridges should you have to go back to them if your buyer backs out at the last minute.

7. Keep emotions in check

I get it, selling your trail book is emotional. It's the culmination of years of hard work and client relationships. But when it's time to sell, treat it as a business transaction. Focus on the numbers and the facts, not your feelings. Again, easier said than done, so have a partner who could be objective. It could be your mentor, key staff member, broker success manager/ partnership manager or a business broker.

It can get overwhelming and drawn-out, and you may get tempted to just get it over with, but don't rush into things without consulting the right team of experts and certainly don't get mad out of frustration at people wanting to help. You only get one chance at this.

8. Be ready to walk away

Don't wait until the last minute to sell your trail book. When your business is at its peak, that's the best time to sell. Walk away on your terms and when you're in control, not when you're desperate. This gives you the power to negotiate and, if needed, step back if the deal doesn't meet your expectations.

Until you've signed anything, you are in charge and hold the power. You can pause discussion and revisit it in a couple of months if life happens and you cannot dedicate the time and energy the sale is demanding.

9. Seek professional advice

Negotiating a trail book sale can be complex, so it's worth consulting professionals. Start with your accountant to ensure the sale fits in to your tax strategy. Then, get in touch with a lawyer to do the contract and set terms. If you can afford a succession or M&A team known within the mortgage broking industry, get them to help you navigate the process. These experts can offer valuable advice, especially since they deal with these kinds of sales every day, but be mindful that they charge like a wounded bull; so if you are just selling the trail book and not the entire business, they should charge accordingly.

Conclusion

Selling your trail book is a huge decision, and it can significantly impact your future. By getting a solid valuation, understanding your buyer and staying flexible during negotiations, you'll be in the best position to secure the right price. Take your time, do your homework and don't be afraid to walk away if the deal isn't right. Remember, the key to getting the best price is being prepared and staying confident. With the right strategy, selling your trail book can be the golden ticket you've been waiting for!

CHAPTER 12

Avoiding the pitfalls: A broker's guide to buying a trail book the smart way

Buying a trail book sounds simple on paper – pay the seller, inherit the clients and enjoy a boost in your passive income. However, like any good business deal, the bigger the potential reward, the greater the risks and responsibilities. I'm not saying that the outgoing brokers are keeping information from you – maybe they are, maybe they aren't – but things rarely go exactly as planned.

My previous employer had a head broker, Suzanne, who had brokers working under her. Before she sold, she did ask them if they wanted to buy the part of the trail they generated. Those brokers said no, but when the trail was advertised for sale, they changed their minds. They wanted to buy their trail back.

Now, Suzanne was friends with this sub-broker wanting to buy their trail book. Post-selling, they would cross paths. Hence, she had to accommodate their request. This delayed the sale. Instead of being able to sell the trail book before the end of the financial year and getting it all in time for taxes, the sale was postponed to the following year. The external buyers had to wait longer and extend the financing they secured from the banks. After the sub-brokers bought their trail, the trail that was now on sale from the head broker was lower, and the shine and excitement were taken away a bit.

If you're a broker thinking of buying a trail book, it's crucial to expect the unexpected so you don't get demotivated and you get the most value out of your investment.

Let's dive into the key things to watch out for, explained simply.

1. Valuation errors

One of the biggest mistakes brokers make is misvaluing the trail book they want to buy. Often, brokers rely on a generic multiplier, like 2x or 3x the annual trail income, without factoring in the quality of the book, client loyalty or future business potential.

Trail book valuers now often call their reports 'business appraisals' rather than 'valuations' because there's more to it than just crunching numbers. If you're buying a trail book that looks great on paper but doesn't have engaged, loyal clients or potential for future growth, you could end up paying more than it's really worth.

Do your homework, ask for detailed metrics and remember: Just because someone says their book sold for 3x, doesn't mean that number applies to every trail book.

2. Not vetting buyers (or sellers)

Not every buyer (or seller) is a good match for the clients in a trail book. If you're buying, it's important to ensure that you are the right person to continue providing the level of service the clients are used to. After all, these clients have been loyal to the broker for years, and the last thing they want is to feel abandoned or mistreated during a transition.

As a seller, if you're not careful about who buys your trail book, you could risk damaging your reputation. Clients will find ways to contact you if the new broker doesn't live up to their expectations, and in today's world of social media, a bad transition can go public quickly. Make sure the buyer is someone with whom you can vibe, reason out and work out a solution when issues arise.

3. Ignoring client relationships

You might be buying the revenue stream, but you're also buying trust. Brokers who fail to introduce themselves properly to the clients they inherit often find that clients leave at a higher rate than expected. We've seen brokers complain of higher runoff after buying a book simply because they didn't take the time to build relationships with the new clients. Even worse, the client wanted to sue the selling broker as her details were passed on to the buying broker, allegedly, without her knowing.

Make sure the seller introduces you to their clients. Once you take over, get to know them. Show genuine interest and keep communication clear. These clients are your new source of income, so treat them well.

4. Overlooking compliance issues

Don't get caught up in the excitement of buying a trail book and ignore the compliance. Some brokers don't do thorough background checks on client files, which can lead to problems later. For example, failing to record clients' goals, purposes or the reasons they sought finance can lead to compliance failures.

Always check that the client files you're acquiring are up to date and compliant with current regulations. In one instance, a client called up the aggregator because she had dragged her broker to court. After which, the broker sold his trail book and went missing in action. The client, then, wanted closure and was enquiring whether the new broker was liable to pay the damages.

5. Neglecting post-sale transition

The sale doesn't end the moment the money changes hands; a smooth transition period is crucial. As a buyer, make sure you get all the personal details (like contact preferences and financial history) and understand each client's future financing needs. If possible, stay involved in an advisory role for a while to make sure the clients feel comfortable.

As a seller, decide beforehand if your phone number is part of the sale. If possible, keep your work number separate from your personal number. If you can't part with the number, the clients will call you and you will have to take on the extra work of redirecting them to the new broker for no extra fee (if not in the contract).

6. Failing to secure confidentiality

Throughout the sales process, you'll be sharing sensitive information about your clients and business. Without proper confidentiality agreements, this data could be misused, leading to legal issues and lost business.

Always ensure that non-disclosure agreements (NDAs) are in place before you begin any serious discussions with potential buyers. Like a marriage certificate, it is just paper; the value lies in trust. Make sure you engage with buyers that your circle of brokers have heard of and know. That way, you know who is looking at your information and trust they will be ethical in their dealings with you. If you aren't sure, the least you can do is redact the loan IDs. Don't give them all the information to recognise the clients easily.

7. Not considering tax implications

Selling or buying a trail book can have big tax implications, so it's critical to speak with an accountant or tax professional before making any moves. Trail books are often a broker's version of a retirement plan, so structuring the deal correctly can help minimise your tax liabilities. This is especially important if you've been avoiding paying into your superannuation and are relying on your trail book for retirement income.

Also, seek investment advice. If you haven't handled so much money before, chances are you may be tempted to spend it irrationally.

8. Read the fine print

Some agreements between brokers and their aggregators may have clauses that affect your ability to sell a trail book. If your clients and trail commissions aren't entirely yours to sell, you could face legal trouble. So, make sure you have permission to transfer these assets before finalising a deal.

Document everything and get your broker agreements and referral agreement reviewed so the trail amount does not differ and create complications. A well-known trail book buyer with over 20 years of industry experience will tell you he knows contracts inside out. He can pull up aggregations on clauses, as he has been reading contracts for years. He is not a solicitor or Justice of Peace, but he knows that the implementation staff are not perfect. Things go wrong. If you are naive enough not to know how contracts differ, you will learn it through making big losses.

9. Lack of clear payment terms

It's amazing how many sales are delayed or fall apart because of unclear payment terms. Agree upfront on how and when the payment will be made, and set a clear settlement date. The agreements team at your aggregator won't decide this for you. It's something you need to work out with the buyer. Get your solicitor to suggest what is to be done. In some instances, money is held in a trust account and paid out gradually, depending on clawback risks.

10. Not having an exit strategy

Whether you're retiring or moving to a new industry, have a clear exit strategy. Knowing the right time to sell and how to maximise the value of your trail book is key. Don't wait until you're desperate to sell; rather, sell when your book is in its best shape so you're in control.

Do an annual review. There are accountants who do an annual sale-ready document, which is akin to an annual health check. You know how it's tracking.

Conclusion

Buying or selling a trail book can be a lucrative way to grow or wind down your business, but it's not without its risks. By avoiding these common pitfalls, you can ensure a smoother transaction that benefits both you and your clients. Always consult with professionals and engage your aggregator, who can help guide you through the process and ensure you're making the right moves at every step.

CHAPTER 13

How to grow profits with old trail books

The Lindy Effect teaches us that 'the longer something has been around, the more likely it will continue to endure'. This insight is especially true for mortgage brokers, particularly when it comes to older trail books. In a short span of time, I've spoken to two veteran brokers looking to sell their businesses – one in Queensland and the other in regional Victoria. These brokers have built extensive networks, still rely on paper-based processes and have minimal digital presence. One even expects a multiple of 3.5x the annual trail, which raises the question: Why would another broker want to buy such a business? Aren't we told that in this digital and AI age only the automated brokerages are more appealing?

The answer is simple: Trust, relationships and sustained value. Older trail books encapsulate decades of client relationships, ethical business practices and resilience in the face of market shifts. These elements hold immense value, often outweighing technology and CRMs in the mortgage broking world.

It may be controversial, but buying a trail book or business from a broker exiting permanently is, in my opinion, the best and hardest trail book to get your hands on. This clean break gives you the peace of mind that the client's loyalties are not being split between two brokers.

Exiting brokers are more motivated to sell quickly and are less concerned with squeezing every dollar out of the deal. Getting hold of such brokers at the right time is the hardest bit; reason being, they try to privately speak to brokers they have in mind to sell to so as not to alarm their clients. People of that generation demonstrate more integrity. Even if another broker comes along with a higher offer, they decide to go with the broker they have spoken with.

Why older trail books are valuable

Established client trust and relationships: Old trail books represent decades of successful relationships, guiding clients (and sometimes their children) through their mortgage journeys. These relationships are incredibly valuable, as they provide instant client bases and established referral networks.

Resilience to market fluctuations: For new brokers, buying an older trail book is like acquiring a business that has stood the test of time. Older brokers have weathered numerous challenges, clawbacks, regulation changes and fluctuating interest rates, and their client bases are loyal.

Operational wisdom: Buying an old trail book allows newer brokers to tap into decades of experience. They gain access to established best practices and strategies for managing client relationships, mitigating risk and navigating regulations.

Brand association: Clients associate trust with a brand or individual. If the outgoing broker is well-regarded, having them remain part of the brand during the transition can help maintain continuity. Whether it's through a formal consultant title or featuring them prominently on social media, keeping the outgoing broker's presence visible can build goodwill.

Risks with poor broker-to-broker dynamics:

Unstable client communication: If there's poor communication between the outgoing and incoming broker, clients may feel unsettled, lose trust and consider switching brokers. For instance, if the outgoing broker always called clients, they should personally introduce the new broker via phone call. Similarly, face-to-face meetings with high-value clients can strengthen the relationship.

Lack of client background: New brokers often miss out if the outgoing broker doesn't transfer essential client information. Even if the data isn't stored in a CRM, at the very least, there should be a list of client names, phone numbers, occupations and loan types.

Mitigating the risks
Mediation for smooth transitions: If the outgoing and incoming brokers have significant differences, consider mediation. Third-party intervention can help align expectations and maintain professional relations.

Contractual clarity: Make sure everything is clearly outlined in the contract – the purchase price, responsibilities, timeline and handover expectations. Leaving things vague increases the likelihood of misunderstandings and failures in the transition.

Detailed transition plan: Develop an offboarding checklist that includes client introductions, transfer of historical client data and a strategy for maintaining continuity in client service.

Conclusion

Buying an older trail book can be incredibly profitable, but don't focus solely on price; instead, foster a positive relationship with the existing broker. If they see that you care about the clients and their legacy, they'll be more inclined to support you even after the deal is done. In contrast, if you approach this as a purely transactional purchase, like buying a second hand car at a bargain, you risk losing the clients who trust the outgoing broker.

If the outgoing broker feels slighted or undervalued, they could quietly steer their clients away from you, and you'd be left with a losing deal. To win with older trail books, you have to use both your head and your heart. That generation was built differently; they still go by feel, get attached, care for things deeply and want to go at a slower pace.

CHAPTER 14

Mastering trail book acquisition: The seven-step blueprint for mortgage brokers

Trail book acquisition is the ultimate strategy for scaling. It is very important to get it right the first time. Things will go wrong, but if the errors are fatal, chances are you will be completely put off purchasing books in the future. Hence, I would suggest to first start with buying a small trail book from within your current aggregator's pool. Your first purchase should not be from another aggregator, as it adds another layer of complexity and steps. Each aggregator uses their own CRM, has a different process and makes it harder for books to leave their portfolios, obviously. Once you get your head around what it entails to acquire a trail book and know the basic structure of what main items need to be ticked off in the checklist, you can do bigger and even risk buying a book from another aggregator next.

Every broker (whether seasoned or new) is eager to buy trail books as a way to fast-track their success, but pace yourself and play it smart. Here are seven critical steps you need to follow to make sure your trail book acquisition is a winning move:

Step 1: Assess the need

Before jumping into buying a trail book, evaluate your current business position. Ask yourself:

- Does this align with my long-term business goals?

- How will this impact my operational capacity?

It's not just about adding more clients or revenue. You also need to deliver consistent value to the clients in the trail book to ensure sustainable growth. Make sure your existing team and processes are ready to handle the increased workload. Don't speak from optimism, but be realistic. It is more work and time than you imagine. It requires a good six weeks for you to correctly onboard the new clients into your ecosystem.

Step 2: Prepare financially

Acquiring a trail book requires a substantial upfront investment. Sellers, especially in today's hot market, expect quick settlements. By understanding all the financial aspects, you minimise risk and ensure the acquisition is a sound investment. You'll need liquidity or financing in place before entering negotiations, and your budget should cover more than just the purchase price. You also need to account for:

- Marketing costs for client outreach.

- Possible attrition or clawbacks due to discharges.

- Operational adjustments, such as hiring additional staff to manage the extra work for the new book of clients.

Step 3: Source opportunities

Finding a trail book is the next step, but it's not as simple as searching on Google. The best opportunities come through networking. Speak up and let people know you are looking to purchase a trail book. Don't be shy to let everyone in the industry know, including lender business development managers. Word spreads fast in this small industry. The beauty of this industry is everyone wants to help. If they come across an opportunity that they cannot take, they may pass it on to you.

Reach out to brokers nearing retirement or those considering a career shift.

Leverage aggregator connections. Often, your BDM knows brokers in their network looking to sell.

Contact business brokers specialising in trail book sales. These professionals can offer a curated list of options and help you negotiate the best deals.

It's critical to verify the reputation of the seller, so only proceed with purchases from brokers known and trusted by either you or your aggregator. Buying from unknown brokers or scammers online can lead to significant issues down the line.

Step 4: Do your due diligence

Due diligence is where you dive deep into the quality of the trail book. Brokers often skip this step, especially in a hot market, but it's essential. Areas to focus on include:

- **Client demographics**: Are they long-term investor clients or just one-time homebuyers?

- **Loan types**: Are they variable-rate loans or fixed-rate loans nearing the end of their term?

- **Compliance history**: Any red flags with lenders or compliance issues could mean trouble for your future cash flow.

Hiring a solicitor with experience in mortgage broking acquisitions to review the contracts and trail book data is a must. A professional will also ensure you have appropriate clauses for clawbacks or lender payments.

Your solicitor has to be someone who has had mortgage broker clients before. Ask the solicitor if you could contact their previous mortgage broker clients so you can speak with them and see how the experience was.

Step 5: Negotiate

Once due diligence is complete, the real work begins – negotiating a fair price. Having a strong negotiating stance while considering future potential will ensure you don't overpay. The value of a trail book is not just based on the commission it generates; it also includes client relationships, future opportunities and potential for expansion. Keep these factors in mind during negotiations and don't be afraid to include terms like:

- **Clawback clauses**: Protect yourself if clients refinance or discharge loans shortly after purchase.

- **Earn-out arrangements**: A portion of the sale price is contingent on future revenue targets being hit.

Step 6: Integrate new clients

Once the deal is done and you've acquired the trail book, your next priority is integrating the new clients into your business. This phase includes:

- **transferring new client data** from the seller's CRM to yours

- **introducing yourself to the clients** via email, phone calls and/or in-person meetings

- **reassuring new clients about continuity** and ensuring them that service levels will remain consistent.

The smoother the transition, the more likely you are to retain the clients and secure the ongoing trail commissions. This is the most painful step, and it will no doubt cause you a lot of frustration and pain if you don't follow up with all parties and get regular updates yourself. There are many fingers in this pie in terms of departments at the aggregators; tasks drop off, and there are delays. If you are aware of this from the start and stay pedantic, you will be able to keep the ball on track.

Step 7: Expand your business

Now that the trail book is part of your business, you can focus on expanding and scaling further. Speak to the outgoing broker to see if their referral partners would continue their referral relationships with you. As a business owner, you cannot afford to be afraid of rejection. Ask, even if the answer could be no. There is no harm in asking. It may be something that a referral partner may not have thought of and may have said yes to avoid disruption to their own business. Use this opportunity to:

- **cross-sell new products**, such as personal or commercial loans, to the existing client base

- **leverage referrals** by asking satisfied clients to introduce friends or family

- **implement proactive customer service strategies** to deepen relationships and generate more loyalty.

Continuous client engagement will help you unlock the full potential of the acquired trail book, ultimately leading to higher profits and business growth.

Conclusion

Following these seven steps ensures you not only purchase a valuable asset but also give the experience and taste to purchase a few more trail books now that you know what's involved.

CHAPTER 15

Making an offer for a trail book: Six key points every mortgage broker must address

Jason had been eyeing trail book acquisitions for a while. His business was growing, he had more than enough cash flow, and he saw an opportunity to fast-track his success by purchasing trail books all over the country, regardless of aggregators. Eager to make his move, Jason rushed into negotiations, as he didn't want to miss out, given trail books are hard to come by.

In his excitement, Jason overlooked some critical steps. He paid 3.2x the trail but found himself in a mess. The commission statements weren't accurate. Some of the trail were recorded as upfront commissions. There were several conditionally approved deals, but the agreement about commission splits wasn't clear. He thought he would be getting half the upfront commission, but after signing the contract, the seller claimed 100% of the work.

Then came the client transition nightmare. The seller had promised a smooth handover but would not show up to client handover meetings. Many clients weren't even aware their loans had been transferred to a new broker. Communication broke down. Within a few months, Jason started noticing a higher-than-expected runoff. Clients were refinancing with other brokers, and clawback provisions kicked in. Jason hadn't secured an escrow fund for potential clawbacks, leaving him financially exposed.

To make matters worse, the CRM system Jason used wasn't compatible with the seller's, forcing his team into a long and manual data entry process to fill in the blanks. By the time they completed the transition, Jason had lost several key clients and was struggling to make the acquisition profitable. He has sworn himself from buying trail books and is now channelling his investment focus into property development instead.

Looking back, Jason realised that rushing the deal without thoroughly addressing key issues was his downfall. If only he had taken the time to consult more experienced brokers, accountants and commission analysers, things could have turned out very differently.

When acquiring a trail book, don't do it alone. Always know of brokers at your aggregator who buy trail books, and make sure to bounce ideas and get tips from them. You don't ask a dentist about knee pain; in the same way, you can't get the best answer from an accountant on a mortgage broking question, especially around commission splits. But speak to your accountant and solicitors too!

Mortgage brokers can easily get bogged down in the details of the transaction, but it's crucial to stay focused on the most important points to ensure the deal works out in your favour, financially and operationally.

Here are six critical aspects to consider when making an offer for a trail book and how each can affect the profitability of the transaction.

1. Multiple of annual trail income

The core value of any trail book lies in its annual trail income – the recurring revenue generated from ongoing client loans. Typically, the purchase price is a multiple of the annual trail, with a 2.5x multiple being a common industry standard. This means that if the trail book generates $100,000 annually, you could be expected to pay around $250,000 for it.

Key consideration:

The multiple reflects not only the income generated from current loans but also future refinancing and repeat business opportunities. Ensure you factor in the sustainability of the book (loan retention rate) when calculating how quickly you can break even and start turning a profit.

2. Referral commission on new clients

A significant part of the growth potential post-acquisition comes from referrals. After acquiring the book, the seller may refer new clients to you. Typically, you offer a 30% commission upfront for these new clients to incentivise the seller to keep sending business your way.

Key consideration:

Ensure that these referral terms are clear and in writing. This could be a golden opportunity to build long-term relationships with the seller's network while expanding your client base.

3. Handling deals in progress

When acquiring a trail book, it's important to account for any deals that are in progress, like:

- **Unconditional deals**: These are fully approved deals that are just waiting to be settled. Sellers usually receive 100% of the upfront commission, as they've done most of the work.

- **Conditionally approved deals**: These deals are still subject to certain conditions. The industry standard is to offer the seller around 50% of the upfront commission, recognising that both parties will put in effort to see the deal through.

Key consideration:
Ensure that all in-progress deals are clearly listed, and clarify who is responsible for following through on each one.

4. Clawback provisions

One of the biggest risks when acquiring a trail book is the possibility of clawbacks when a client refinances or pays off their loan early, resulting in the lender taking back a portion of the commission.

Protect yourself. It's standard practice to retain 10% of the purchase price in escrow for 12 months to cover potential clawbacks. This safety net ensures you don't suffer financially if clients refinance soon after the purchase.

Key consideration:

Ensure this is clearly outlined in the contract and negotiated upfront to avoid misunderstandings later.

5. Transition period and client communication

A seamless transition is key to retaining clients post-acquisition. Often, the seller will stay on temporarily to reassure clients about the change and offer continuity.

- **Personal communication**: The seller should send out initial communications, including emails or phone calls, to introduce you as the new broker. Joint communications from both parties can make clients feel more comfortable.

- **Maintaining accreditation**: In some cases, the seller may remain accredited under your brand to handle administrative tasks like loan repricing at no additional cost to you.

Key consideration:
Clear and consistent communication with clients is essential. Set clear expectations for the seller's involvement during the transition period, and ensure both parties agree on how and when clients will be informed.

6. Operational handover

To operate smoothly post-acquisition, you need all relevant client data before the settlement date:

- **Client list**: Ensure you receive a full client contact list with key details like contact information, loan types and pipeline deals.

- **Manual transition**: Depending on the CRM system being used, manual data entry might be necessary. Allow sufficient time to ensure all information are accurately transferred.

Key consideration:
The quality of the data you receive can directly affect how quickly you can start generating revenue from the acquired book. Get access to the data as early as possible so that you can prepare.

Now, if you do decide to buy your trail book from selling portals, which have the ability to source, negotiate and settle transactions, it does take some of the stress away. They provide the contracts, do the due diligence, lodge the transfer paperwork and do the follow ups – not to the extent you would provide if you knew what to look for and how to do the checks.

The catch, however, is that you don't have a personal relationship with the seller during the process, and some of your questions will go unanswered. You may also be competing with a whole lot more brokers for the sale trail books, overpay for the book and miss requesting compliance check records directly from the seller. Whilst you don't get to pick up the phone and call, you are able to make enquiries using the links next to the listings.

Conclusion

When acquiring a trail book, understanding the financial intricacies is critical to the long-term profitability of the deal. By focusing on these six key points, from calculating the purchase price to ensuring a smooth client transition, you can ensure that your investment will deliver returns.

CHAPTER 16

The three-step communication strategy for seamless trail book integration

Acquiring a trail book presents an incredible opportunity for business owners to expand their client base and service portfolio. However, transitioning these clients into your business can be challenging without an effective communication strategy. The key is to build trust quickly, ensure clients are informed and integrate them smoothly into your existing operations. Call upon every team involved at your current aggregator and the other aggregator (if applicable).

Get to know your state team, agreements team and the commissions team, in particular. They are the three main departments that can escalate and provide answers on anything and everything CRM. At the same time, don't rely on things to work themselves out. Departments have extremely busy days and some quiet days. They also have blackout days prior to the end of the financial year to calibrate.

The date on which the sale of your trail book will settle depends when your deal hits their inbox. If it is during the busy periods, it may be sent at the back of the line, delaying settlement by a month or two. You may not be notified, and you will be disappointed if you left the follow-up for the last minute.

This simple yet powerful three-step communication strategy helps brokers succeed when acquiring a new trail book.

Step 1: Data segmentation and tagging

The foundation of any effective communication strategy lies in how well you understand and organise your client data. Before integrating the new trail book into your CRM, it's essential to acquire a comprehensive client list, including any unique CRM IDs or existing tags. Organising clients by categories (such as loan type, settlement date or business type) allows for targeted communication.

Why is this important?

Client segmentation helps you tailor your messaging. Not all clients are at the same stage of their mortgage journey, and some may need more attention than others. For example, you may need a separate approach for clients with settled loans versus those whose loans are due for review. Tagging clients properly ensures they receive information relevant to them, leading to a smoother transition and building trust.

How to implement:

- Collaborate with your aggregator's BDM to transfer and map the client data into your CRM.

- Create tags such as 'Business Newsletters', 'Settled {Month} – Active Loan' or 'Postcode {Month} – Contact' to ensure the right communication reaches the right client.

- Regularly update and clean your data to maintain accuracy and relevance.

Step 2: Personalised introductions

Once the data is segmented, your next move is to introduce yourself to your newly acquired clients. The first email or communication sets the tone for the future relationship. Sending a personalised email ensures clients feel valued and well-informed about the change.

Why is this important?

Clients need reassurance that their financial journey is in safe hands. A formal and thoughtful introduction eases any potential concerns, and personalisation adds a human touch to the process, making clients feel like more than just a number.

How to implement:

- Use segmented email lists to send personalised introductions. For example, clients tagged 'Settlement {Month} – Contact' should receive an email relevant to their most recent settlement date.

Employ an automated follow-up system. If an email remains unopened after two days, resend it with a different subject line to ensure it reaches the client.

Schedule a second touchpoint six months later to check in, providing a consistent and caring service experience.

Step 3: Direct outreach via SMS and calls

In today's fast-paced digital world, clients often miss emails or avoid phone calls. To combat this, SMS messaging is a highly effective method of getting your message across instantly. Short and concise, SMS lets clients know that you're available and ready to help. That does not mean you won't attempt to reach them on the phone. If they don't answer, the SMS will let them know why you rang and coax them to respond.

Why is this important?
Clients appreciate proactive brokers who prioritise their needs. Offering a loan health check or information about refinancing through SMS shows you are dedicated to providing ongoing value. It's also a way to interact with clients who may not be immediately responsive to emails or calls.

How to implement:
- Send SMS updates to clients with personalised messages that offer services like a loan review. Keep the message short and direct.

- Use a system that allows clients to reply with simple responses such as 'Yes' for an appointment or follow-up. This increases engagement.

- If possible, schedule direct calls to high-value clients for a more personalised touch. Take them out to a nice business lunch and give them extra attention in exchange for the bigger loans they may retain with you. Direct conversations foster stronger relationships and help build rapport faster.

Conclusion

Acquiring a trail book is only the beginning. The success of integrating new clients into your business lies in your ability to communicate effectively and build trust quickly. By segmenting client data, sending personalised introductions and implementing direct outreach strategies through SMS and calls, brokers can foster loyalty and ensure their new clients feel valued and cared for. These structured communication strategies will ensure that clients transition smoothly while helping your brokerage stand out as one that prioritises service, care and ongoing support.

CHAPTER 17

Financing the trail book purchase: What you need to know

I went through a lot in the previous chapters, and I am aware that we didn't touch on the pain point much – the money to buy. This is no doubt the most important element of the deal.

Most trail books get snapped up within a week or two due to the high demand in the market, so brokers need to have financing ready when the opportunity arises – and big brokers have the funds sitting in the business, ready to go. No doubt they will purchase these books to feed the other non-lead-generating brokers in the business. In order to stay in competition, you need to have the funds ready to go too. No matter how nice or professional you are, if you are not finance-ready, no seller will entertain you, especially when 90% of brokers are ready to buy. You need to have the money conversation upfront.

If you're not sitting on large sums of liquid cash, securing financing is essential to stay competitive. Like we touched on in previous chapters, you can work out an arrangement with your head broker, real estate agent or guarantor if buying a book is a pressing matter for you.

Now, securing finance for a trail book purchase involves meticulous preparation and thorough documentation. Lenders require detailed information about your business's past performance and projections as well as a complete picture of your financial health and the potential of the trail book you wish to buy. So, keep your accountant close but your bookkeeper closer, and ensure all your documentation are in order and have no gaps or missing pieces that could make the deal fall through.

In this chapter, I'll walk you through the key steps and essential documentation needed to successfully apply for financing to buy a trail book. Whether you're new to trail book purchases or a seasoned broker looking to expand understanding, this process will help ensure you're fully prepared to acquire that valuable asset.

Start with a business plan outlining an overview of your business, your experience in financial services, competitive landscape, cash flow projections from the trail book, loan repayment plan and details on your existing trail book should you be using that as collateral.

10 essential documents you need for financing

Trail book acquisitions often involve significant sums, commonly $2 million and up, and lenders need assurance that the purchase is a sound investment both for you and for them. They want to mitigate their risk, so they'll scrutinise your financial health and the viability of the trail book being acquired. The better prepared you are with these documentations, the quicker you'll secure financing.

Application form & personal financial overview

Lenders need to evaluate your overall financial standing. They will require you to fill out an application and provide a detailed overview of your personal assets and liabilities, much like they would ask your clients when applying for home loans. Review your personal expenses and income carefully before applying, as lenders will scrutinise every detail.

Profit and Loss (P&L) and cash flow projections in the next three years

Lenders will assess how stable and sustainable your revenue is based on your projections. This shows lenders your business's financial growth potential and current profit levels. Break down your income from upfront commissions, trails, referral fees and any other earnings.

P&L statements for past financial years

Past performance matters. Your business's financial track record provides lenders with insights into your stability. Make sure all your financials are accurate, updated and complete to avoid delays in the approval process.

Personal tax returns

Lenders will look at both your business and personal financial health. They'll request personal tax returns for all directors and their spouses to assess total household income and ensure you have the capacity to repay the loan.

Business account bank statements for the last six months

Recent bank statements offer a snapshot of your current cash flow and business activity. Lenders want to see regular income inflows and responsible financial management.

Australian Taxation Office (ATO) portals of all directors and spouses for the last 12 months

Lenders want reassurance that your business is up to date with tax obligations, and ATO records show your tax compliance and overall financial transparency.

Commission statements for the last 12 months

This gives lenders a detailed view of your income streams and whether they are consistent, reflecting your ability to maintain repayments on the loan.

Certified ID for all directors

Identification verification is a basic but essential part of the lending process. Lenders need certified copies of identification for all directors to prevent fraud.

Background on business and directors

Lenders are interested in the experience, expertise and background of the business owners. They'll want to see a history of strong leadership and successful business management, which will give them confidence that the business will continue to thrive after the acquisition.

Loan book analysis (LBA)

The LBA is a crucial part of the due diligence process. It provides a detailed analysis of the trail book's performance, including loan sizes, client demographics, runoff rates and any potential risks. This is where the real value of the trail book is assessed, and it's essential for lenders to determine the book's worth.

Conclusion

Buying a trail book is a huge step in scaling your mortgage broking business, but financing it requires careful preparation. Having these 10 documents ready and up to date will streamline the process and give you the best chance of securing the funding you need. Remember, lenders are in the business of risk management, and presenting them with a complete financial picture shows them that you're a low-risk, high-reward borrower.

Always consult with your BDM and aggregator for additional support when navigating the documentation and loan application process. The more prepared you are, the faster you can jump on the next trail book opportunity that comes your way.

CHAPTER 18

Understanding TOFA's impact on trail book purchases for mortgage brokers

For mortgage brokers eager to acquire or sell trail books, it's essential to understand how tax regulations like the **Taxation of Financial Arrangements (TOFA)** can impact transactions.

The TOFA rules aim to better align the tax treatment of financial gains and losses with the economic reality of those transactions. This is especially relevant for large trail books where significant monthly recurring revenue (over $15,000) can trigger TOFA regulations. These rules are not always top of mind, yet they can substantially impact the timing of income recognition and tax liabilities. For trail book purchasers and sellers, these rules can have direct consequences on tax planning. Brokers need to carefully structure these deals not only to optimise income but also to manage tax liabilities effectively.

How TOFA affects trail book purchases

Most brokers focus on acquiring trail books to increase revenue streams, but they often overlook how TOFA can impact their financial planning. By understanding how TOFA affects a mortgage broking business, brokers can better navigate the complexities of these large financial transactions.

1. Income recognition

TOFA requires brokers to recognise income when it is **earned**, not necessarily when it is **received**. For trail books generating substantial monthly commissions, this means that the income needs to be declared when it accrues, even if the payment comes in later.

> **Example**: If a broker's trail book generates $18,000 per month but receives the actual payment in the following month (July), the broker is required to recognise that income in June's fiscal year – FY2024, not FY2025.

Impact: Brokers may have to pay taxes on income before it is actually received, which could affect cash flow and financial planning.

2. Hedging against income variability

For brokers dealing with large trail books, fluctuations in interest rates or client refinancing can impact income like it is currently. TOFA allows brokers to hedge against these risks using financial instruments like swaps. These instruments smooth out income variability.

Example: If a broker anticipates that falling interest rates might reduce the trail income, they could use a derivative contract to hedge against that loss. Under TOFA, any gains or losses from this hedging activity would be recognised in the same period as the corresponding trail income.

Impact: This allows the broker to manage tax impacts more effectively by timing gains or losses to match changes in their trail income.

3. Valuation of trail books

When dealing with large trail books, TOFA also influences how these financial assets are valued. The book must be assessed at fair value, which means its future cash flows need to be discounted to present value.

Example: A broker selling a trail book worth $1 million must adjust the book's value according to factors like client defaults, discharges or interest rate changes.

Impact: Regular revaluations can affect reported income and tax obligations in any given fiscal year.

4. Deferral and spreading provisions

TOFA allows for deferral and spreading of income, which is particularly beneficial for brokers receiving large lump sums from trail book purchases or sales.

Example: If a broker sells part of their trail book and receives a lump sum of $200,000, TOFA rules may allow that income to be spread over multiple years, reducing the one-time tax hit.

Impact: Spreading income over several years can smooth out tax liabilities, reducing the impact of one-time large payments.

Conclusion

TOFA introduces complexities into the buying and selling of trail books, particularly when dealing with significant monthly commission streams. Consulting with a tax professional is highly recommended to ensure compliance and to optimise tax strategies when navigating trail book transactions.

Pro Tip: Always work with a qualified tax accountant who can help you structure your trail book purchase in a tax-efficient way, ensuring you're aware of TOFA's potential impact on your transaction.

CHAPTER 19

Avoiding buyer's remorse: Common complaints when purchasing trail books

For mortgage brokers looking to scale quickly, buying a trail book is made to seem like a no-brainer. It's a shortcut to increasing revenue and growing your business without the long and slow grind of acquiring new clients. As I've mentioned before, 'it's faster to buy profits than to earn them organically'. However, not all trail book purchases are smooth sailing. Brokers often encounter several unexpected challenges post-purchase, which can turn what seemed like a golden opportunity into a headache. Go in with the mindset that things will go wrong, and you will be prepared come what may.

You cannot avoid detours no matter how prepared you are, and it hurts more if you go through it all by yourself. So, surround yourself with a team of professionals – an aggregator contact who knows all the lenders on your side, an accountant who is a business adviser, and a solicitor who knows how to keep you legally safe and can take action should the buyer breach terms or violate your trust.

Let's dive into the most common complaints mortgage brokers have after buying a trail book and how you can avoid them.

1. Hidden risks

One of the biggest issues brokers face when purchasing trail books is hidden risks. A trail book might look great on paper, but there are always details beneath the surface that could impact its value. For instance, many trail books contain a large number of fixed-rate loans, which are less likely to be refinanced in the near term.

If you inherit a trail book full of clients on fixed rates, you might struggle to refinance them, limiting your income potential. Most buyers get an independent expert to analyse their trail book by reviewing year-on-year commission statements to assess its value at a specific point in time.

Solution:
Always ask the seller or aggregator for a thorough LBA document that outlines not just the financial data but the non-financial metrics too. You'll want to know the loan types, loan maturity and risk factors before sealing the deal.

2. Tax implications

A trail book purchase is considered a capital expense, and this comes with certain tax consequences. While the purchase price might be high (often starting at $150,000, and going up to $7 million for large books), the runoff rate can be significant. Currently, runoffs are around 20%; meaning that if you do nothing, the income from the book could diminish rapidly within just four years.

Solution:
Consult with an accountant before making the purchase to understand the long-term tax implications and depreciation rules for trail books. Knowing your true **return on investment (ROI)** is critical when making such a large outlay.

3. Professional indemnity (PI) coverage

There's a widespread misconception that the newly acquired trail book will automatically be covered by your existing professional indemnity (PI) policy. However, the reality is that you may need to extend your PI coverage to include the potential liabilities associated with the previous broker's work. Similarly, the seller should maintain run-off cover on their PI policy to cover any historical issues.

Solution: Have an insurance expert review the trail book purchase agreement to ensure that both your PI and the seller's PI are in good standing.

4. Clawback risks

One of the scariest risks in buying a trail book is clawbacks – when the lender requires repayment of commission because a loan is paid out early or refinanced. Some brokers churn their book right before selling, leaving the buyer to deal with clawbacks.

Solution:
Ensure that the sale agreement includes a clawback clause. This typically means withholding a portion of the sale price (up to 10% to 20%) for a year or two after the sale to cover potential clawbacks. Always get

the agreement reviewed by a solicitor experienced in mortgage broking to protect yourself from this risk.

5. Legal complications

Buying a trail book isn't as simple as handing over the money and getting the clients. There are legal approvals needed, especially from the aggregator under which the seller operates. If the selling broker was part of an aggregation agreement, the buying broker needs to understand the net trail income split and confirm which files are part of the sale (settled loans, pre-approved applications, etc.).

Solution:
Work with a lawyer to draft a Deed of Assignment and ensure all legalities are taken care of. The more comprehensive the legal documentation, the smoother the transition.

6. Valuation: Is the trail book really worth what you're paying?

Getting an independent valuation of the trail book is critical. Without it, you might overpay for a book that doesn't deliver the expected returns. Aggregators often provide an Information Memorandum or Loan Book

Valuation document that helps justify the price using data analytics from their CRMs to evaluate the true value of the book.

Solution:
Spend the $2,000 to $4,000 on an independent valuation to ensure you're paying a fair price. Don't just take the seller's word for it; get an objective data-driven analysis.

7. Scams

As with any financial transaction, there's a risk of scams. Fake brokers or unscrupulous sellers may advertise trail books to lure in buyers only to disappear once they've received a deposit.

Solution:
Before agreeing to any transaction, ensure the seller's reputation is verified. Ask for references from other brokers or consult industry forums to check if the seller is genuine. Never transfer money without performing due diligence.

8. Client transition

A key challenge post-purchase is ensuring a smooth client transition. If the selling broker hasn't maintained accurate client records or doesn't use a CRM system, you may inherit a book with missing contact details, making it difficult to connect with clients. This lack of communication can lead to client dissatisfaction and runoff.

Solution:

Ensure that the seller provides full access to client records including mobile numbers and emails. You should also have a plan to engage these clients early, introduce yourself and establish a rapport to prevent them from leaving.

Conclusion

Purchasing a trail book is not without its risks. From hidden pitfalls to tax implications, PI coverage and client transition issues, it's critical that you do your homework before making such a significant investment. By understanding and mitigating these common complaints you'll be better prepared to make an informed decision and maximise your returns.

Remember: A well-planned purchase can set you on the path to sustainable, long-term growth, but a poorly executed one can lead to costly regrets. Take your time, consult with the right professionals and ensure every aspect of the deal is clear before you commit.

Recap of Section 2: Power of trail books

Chapter 6: Boosting the value of your trail book

- Plan three months to five years ahead to prepare your trail book for sale.

- Use your CRM reports to track key non-financial metrics.

- Block an hour weekly for CRM updates to ensure data accuracy.

- Track performance metrics to create an appealing asset for potential buyers.

Chapter 7: Getting the right price

- Aim for 3x to 3.7x, based on your book's quality.

- Focus on compliance and retention to improve your valuation multiple.

- Review the lifecycle stage (startup, growth, decline or maturity) to adjust expectations.

Chapter 8: Buying a trail book

- Assess multiple potential revenue streams for passive income to cover costs in slow months.

- Integrate the acquired clients into your existing operations.

- Identify potential for offering additional services (e.g., commercial, asset finance or personal loans).

Chapter 9: Valuing your trail book

- Use multiple valuation methods to assess worth.

- Understand your client demographics to justify the valuation.

- Ensure costs of maintaining the trail book are reflected in the final valuation.

Chapter 10: Guide for new brokers

- Explore profit sharing and joint ventures with real estate agents or investors.

- Understand loan book analysis and commission statements.

- Build one-on-one rapport with acquired clients to increase retention.

Chapter 11: Selling your trail book

- Use financial and non-financial data to justify your asking price.

- Negotiate flexible terms for a smoother sale.

- Cultivate controlled competition (maximum of five prospects) to increase your leverage during negotiations.

Chapter 12: Smart trail book acquisition

- Don't overlook due diligence to examine financials, commission statements and client base.

- Document responsibilities and expectations with the selling broker.

- Ensure regular, biannual communication with clients post-acquisition.

Chapter 13: Growing profits with old trail books

- Build client relationships with the next generation of clients related to the older clients.

- Add technology and adopt processes to seamlessly onboard clients from older books.

- Focus on client retention strategies to offset potential runoff from ageing books.

Chapter 14: Seven-step trail book acquisition blueprint

- Ensure your team can manage the increased workload.

- Arrange financing before entering negotiations to act quickly on opportunities.

- Cross-sell and create more opportunities for referrals from the acquired book.

Chapter 15: Making an offer

- Align your offer based on industry-standard multiples.

- Ensure clear terms for both old and new client referrals from the seller.

- Include clawback provisions in contracts to protect against early client refinancing.

Chapter 16: Communication for client integration

- Tag and categorise clients in the CRM to tailor communication during the transition.

- Call and send personalised emails to introduce yourself as the new broker.

- Recognise and appreciate your high-value clients with preferential treatment and exclusive service.

Chapter 17: Financing the purchase

- Organise key financial documents (P&Ls, balance sheets and tax returns) for lenders.

- Understand the trail book's future revenue potential to structure your financing.

- Work with tax professionals to structure your finances prior to purchase.

Chapter 18: Understanding TOFA

- Recognise trail book income when earned, not when received.

- Use hedging to manage income variability (large trail books).

- Explore deferral options under TOFA to manage large upfront payments.

Chapter 19: Avoiding buyer's remorse

- Investigate hidden risks by speaking to the seller over a casual coffee catch-up.

- Ensure proper PI coverage for acquired books and seller's runoff cover.

- Ensure smooth handover of client relationships to retain value post-purchase.

CHAPTER 20

Brokerage's finances: A simple and strategic chart of accounts

Rebecca had been a self-employed mortgage broker for five years, thriving on her natural ability to connect with clients and close deals. When tax season rolled around, she felt lost. Like many brokers, she relied heavily on her accountant and bookkeeper to handle the numbers, only glancing at her P&L statement and balance sheet when required. It worked until it didn't.

During one of our Profit sessions with her, we pointed out a few discrepancies in her records that flagged potential issues with the ATO. Her bookkeeper had miscategorised some expenses and unknowingly overstated her revenue. These errors led to a small audit.

She wasn't fined heavily, but the stress and time wasted navigating the mess, re-coding transactions and creating journals taught her a valuable lesson. It became clear to Rebecca that she couldn't afford to be disconnected from the financial side of her business any longer. She realised that if she had better control over her **chart of accounts (COA)** and understood how to read her P&L and balance sheet, she could prevent future issues, track her progress and make smarter business decisions. The thought of looking through Xero, the accounting software, regularly felt overwhelming at first, but she knew it was crucial for long-term success.

As a self-employed mortgage broker, knowing the ins and outs of your finances is crucial for running a successful business. Yet, many brokers rely heavily on their accountants and bookkeepers to handle their financial records, often remaining disconnected from their own P&L statements and balance sheets. They don't even know how to read these two important financial health check documents.

Some brokers who do their own bookkeeping make mistakes, and that could flag issues in their P&L and balance sheet. Some errors may not be obvious to you, but to a seasoned accountant, they will pick it up in a few minutes. This could result in you being fined by the ATO and wasting money in penalties. To avoid all the hassle, get it right from the start and have the functional ability to read your own P&L and balance sheets.

That said, understanding your finances doesn't need to be overwhelming. It can be as simple as stepping on a digital scale that gives you your weight, BMI and fat index all on one screen. It's about seeing the numbers that matter, quickly and clearly.

In this chapter, we'll break down how to use an ideal COA tailored for mortgage brokers, providing transparency and control over your finances. By organising your financial data effectively, you can benchmark your performance, optimise tax planning and make strategic business decisions with ease.

What is a chart of accounts?

A chart of accounts (COA) is an organised list of all the accounts used by a business to record its financial transactions. Think of it as the financial backbone of your brokerage, categorising all income, expenses, assets and liabilities into neat sections. For mortgage brokers, a properly structured COA can help you track commissions, client incentives, referral fees, operational costs and much more. An effective COA allows you to:

- monitor financial performance clearly
- ensure tax compliance and reduce liabilities benchmark your business against industry standards
- identify areas where you can improve profitability.

Below, we'll go through the key sections of an ideal COA for mortgage brokers.

Revenue section (200 Series)

The revenue section of your COA should reflect the different types of income your brokerage earns. Breaking these down into categories makes it easier to track where your money is coming from.

Residential/commercial/asset finance upfront commissions (200, 205, 210):

Create distinct accounts for the upfront commissions from residential loans, commercial loans and asset finance. This allows you to see which part of your business is bringing in the most revenue. For instance, if your residential upfront commissions are higher than commercial, you can focus on growing your commercial deals to balance your income streams.

Trail commissions (215):

Track your ongoing trail commissions from settled loans. This is the lifeblood of any brokerage and essential for long-term income.

Referral revenue (220-224):

Keep separate accounts for referral income from insurance, financial planning and concierge services. Each referral stream should be tracked individually for clarity.

Brokerage and consulting revenue (230, 235):

If your brokerage offers additional services like consulting or advisory services, log these earnings separately.

Other income (250 Series):

Include any incidental income, like interest earned, fringe benefits tax (FBT) contributions or profits from selling assets.

Cost of goods sold (COGS) section (300 Series)

The **COGS** section records the direct costs associated with delivering your services. For mortgage brokers, these are typically fees related to commission splits and client incentives.

Aggregator fees and clawbacks (300, 301):

Track the fees paid to your aggregator and any clawback costs you incur from commissions that need to be refunded. For instance, if a client refinances within a year, you might face a clawback. Recording these helps you clearly see the real cost of certain deals.

Commission costs (305-310):

Record any commissions paid to contractor brokers or introducers who refer clients to you. This is critical in understanding the cost of acquiring new clients.

Client and operational expenses (315-330):

This includes client incentives, valuation fees and other direct operational costs. You want a detailed view of these to ensure you're not overspending on client acquisition.

Operating expenses section (400 Series)

Your operating expenses are the day-to-day costs of running your brokerage. These are not directly tied to specific deals but are critical in keeping the lights on and your team productive.

Technology expenses (410, 438, 474):

Include expenses for your CRM systems, loan processing software and any other digital tools that help you run your brokerage smoothly.

Staff costs (406, 417, 420, 475-478):

This section should cover employee wages, contractor fees, bonuses and any benefits. Even if you start as a one-person operation, tracking these expenses becomes essential as your team grows.

Premises expenses (408, 445, 462, 469, 470):
Rent, utilities, office supplies and insurance fall under this category. If you're working from a home office, make sure to track the portion of these costs that are tax-deductible.

The importance of benchmarking your COA

One of the biggest advantages of having a well-structured COA is the ability to benchmark your brokerage against industry peers. This means comparing your financial performance with other brokers in your aggregator group, state- or business-size. Benchmarking helps you understand how well you're doing, where you need to improve and how you stack up against your competitors.

By keeping your COA consistent and detailed, you can compare:

- **revenue per broker** (how much each team member generates)

- **average deal size** and profitability by loan type

- **operational efficiency** by comparing costs like rent, wages and marketing against industry standards.

Pro Tip: Speak to your BDM at your aggregator for access to benchmarking tools and COA templates.

Actionable takeaways

1. **Split your revenue categories** between upfront commissions, trail commissions and referral fees to better understand your income sources.

2. **Track costs** associated with aggregators, clawbacks and client incentives carefully to avoid overspending.

3. **Use your COA to benchmark** your brokerage's performance against others in your industry, helping you spot growth opportunities and areas for improvement.

With the right COA in place, you can quickly see where your brokerage financially stands, just like stepping on a digital scale to measure your progress. By keeping things simple, clear and strategic, you'll have the confidence to drive your business forward.

Conclusion

A well-organised COA is more than just an accounting tool. It's a strategic advantage for your mortgage brokerage. By clearly defining your revenue streams, expenses and operational costs, you'll gain deeper insights into your business's performance. This knowledge allows you to make informed decisions, optimise your spending and ultimately increase your profitability.

CHAPTER 21

Why must you prioritise net profit over gross revenue?

Many mortgage broker business owners have their own systems to track performance, often focusing on gross commissions and revenue. To truly understand the health and potential of a brokerage, it's essential to look beyond top-line numbers and pay close attention to net profit, the actual amount left after all expenses (operating costs, commission splits, marketing expenses, rent, salaries and taxes) are deducted.

A brokerage bringing in large commissions but spending too much on overheads is not as successful as a small and leaner operation with a healthier profit margin. Net profit is a key indicator of long-term value and can give you a better business valuation

In this chapter, we'll dive into why net profit should be your primary metric for success and how focusing on it can boost your business's sustainability, growth and resilience.

Gross revenue vs. net profit

Many brokers celebrate their gross commissions or total revenue, but it only tells part of the story. It doesn't account for the many operational costs that can erode your earnings, such as staffing, compliance, marketing, aggregator fees and technology subscriptions.

> **Gross commissions**: Your brokerage's total earnings before subtracting any costs or fees.

> **Net profit**: What remains after all costs – like rent, employee wages, aggregator fees, compliance costs and others – are deducted from the gross commissions.

Case study 1: From struggles to stability

Take the case of a Melbourne brokerage generating $1.5 million in annual gross commissions. While impressive on paper, the brokerage was barely breaking even with a net profit margin of 5%. The root cause? High office rent and an underperforming marketing strategy.

Here's how the brokerage turned things around:

- They switched to a coworking space, reducing office expenses by 25%.

- They refined their marketing strategy, focusing on targeted content that resonated with their ideal clients.

Outcome:
These adjustments helped increase their net profit margin from **5% to 12%**, allowing the brokerage to retain more earnings and reinvest in better growth strategies.

The true cost of operations

It's not just the obvious costs, like rent and wages, that affect your net profit. In fact, many costs are hidden, such as aggregator fees, compliance costs and training. Here are just some of the common expenses mortgage brokers overlook:

- **Aggregator and Australian Credit Licence (ACL) fees**: Fees to maintain your licensing or aggregator services can be substantial.

- **Technology and subscription costs**: Tools like CRMs, compliance platforms and loan origination systems can eat into profits.

- **Marketing and lead generation**: The cost of maintaining visibility and attracting leads can skyrocket if not carefully monitored.

Case study 2: Leveraging technology to improve net profit

A Sydney-based brokerage was seeing a shrinking net profit despite strong gross revenue due to high lead acquisition costs. So, they **implemented ApplyOnline**, a digital compliance tool that automated document collection and loan submission processes. This led to:

- 15% reduction in compliance costs
- 20% faster loan processing times, improving client satisfaction and reducing the need for additional staff.

Outcome:

These process improvements directly enhanced their net profit, helping them operate more efficiently without compromising on quality or service.

Reinvesting in growth

A focus on net profit gives you the flexibility to reinvest earnings back into your business for growth and long-term stability. This can mean hiring new staff, upgrading technology or even expanding geographically.

Case study 3: Profit discipline pays off

A small mortgage brokerage in Brisbane aimed to keep 15% of revenue as profit to create a financial buffer. This discipline allowed the brokerage to acquire a competitor's trail book when the market softened, effectively doubling their client base and boosting long-term profits.

Outcome:

The brokerage saw consistent growth in revenue while maintaining financial stability, ensuring they could weather market downturns and continue expanding.

The benefits of focusing on net profit

A healthy net profit margin doesn't just help keep your business afloat; it enables you to scale, invest in new markets or hire better staff. When you prioritise profit retention, you can:

- acquire more trail books or invest in joint ventures to expand your reach

- build better teams by investing in training and development, creating a competitive advantage
- reinvest in your business, whether through new technologies, marketing campaigns or geographic expansion.

Conclusion

The key takeaway for mortgage brokers is to focus on net profit rather than getting distracted by gross revenue. Understanding and improving your net profit will set you apart from the brokers who focus only on top-line earnings. It is more about the financial rewards than the awards.

By regularly reviewing your expenses, streamlining processes and reinvesting profits wisely, you can ensure sustainable growth in your business. Small, consistent changes can compound over time, creating a stronger foundation for long-term success.

CHAPTER 22

Mastering EBITDA: Key to understanding your brokerage's financial health

When you think about the financial health of your mortgage broking business, **EBITDA** might sound like just another buzzword. It's actually one of the most useful tools in your financial toolkit. **EBITDA** stands for **earnings before interest, taxes, depreciation and amortisation**. Your business is the whole cake before you start cutting each of those letters, aka expenses, away. For the data nerds, yes, I refer to the pie chart.

It's a metric that allows you to measure how well your business is performing from its core operations. By focusing on the revenue you generate from facilitating loans and managing clients without getting bogged down in non-operating expenses, you can get a much clearer view of how profitable your business really is.

Let's dive into how EBITDA can benefit your business and why it's a key metric for mortgage brokers.

Understanding EBITDA

In a mortgage broking business, revenue comes from two main sources – upfront commissions when a loan is settled, and trail commissions as long as the client stays with the lender. These commissions are the lifeblood of your business. Now, EBITDA helps you understand just how well your brokerage is doing and how well your mortgage broking activities are performing by focusing on operational profitability and stripping out non-operating and non-cash expenses.

For instance, if you facilitate a $1 million mortgage, you may earn an upfront commission of **0.65%** (that's $6,500). Over time, as the loan remains active, you'll continue to earn a trail commission of **0.15%** annually.

EBITDA helps you look at this revenue stream without getting distracted by taxes, interest payments or depreciation so you can focus on the numbers that matter most – the money your core business generates.

Benchmarking your performance

EBITDA is a great way to compare your brokerage's performance against competitors. If two brokers generate the same revenue but have different EBITDA figures, it means their operational efficiency and cost structures vary. By analysing your EBITDA, you can pinpoint where you might be overspending and where there's room for improvement.

Imagine two mortgage brokers both facilitate $30 million in mortgages per year. Broker A has an EBITDA of $500,000, while Broker B has an EBITDA of $750,000. Despite having the same revenue, Broker B is operating more efficiently and their business is generating more profit from core operations.

This insight can drive you to optimise your own costs and boost profitability.

Debt servicing

As a small business owner, you may have taken out loans to grow your brokerage. One of the key advantages of EBITDA is that it shows how well your business can handle debt servicing. If your EBITDA is high compared to your interest obligations, you're in a good position to cover your debts without stress.

For example, if your brokerage has an EBITDA of $500,000 and annual interest payments of $100,000, you're comfortably covering your interest obligations, leaving you with room to reinvest in your business. This means you can take on debt for future growth with confidence, knowing your core business can support it.

Valuation and investment

If you're thinking about expanding or bringing in external investment, EBITDA is one of the first metrics that investors will look at. They want to see a business that has consistent and healthy operational earnings, and a higher EBITDA signals that your business is well-run and efficient, making it more attractive for potential partners, investors or even buyers.

For instance, if you're considering a joint venture with a real estate agency, they'll look at your EBITDA to assess your business's profitability and whether you're a good partner for growth. A high EBITDA will also give you leverage in negotiations.

Liquidity assessment

One of the main reasons to focus on EBITDA is to get a better understanding of your business's liquidity, which refers to the cash you have available to run your business day-to-day. By looking at EBITDA, you can assess how much cash your business generates from operations, which is crucial for covering operating expenses like wages, rent and marketing.

For example, a fictional mortgage broking firm, Loans Ahoy, based in Bendigo has a total revenue of $1 million from commissions. After accounting for salaries, rent and marketing expenses, they have an EBITDA of $450,000. This figure shows that the business is generating solid cash flow from its core operations, making it easier to plan for future growth and manage day-to-day operations.

How to calculate EBITDA

Let's break it down for a mortgage broking business:

- **Total revenue** (upfront and trail commissions): $1,000,000
- **Wages and salaries**: $400,000
- **Rent and utilities**: $100,000
- **Marketing expenses**: $50,000

- **Depreciation**: $20,000
- **Interest payments**: $30,000

To calculate EBITDA, you focus only on operating expenses:

$$EBITDA = Total\ Revenue - (Wages + Rent + Marketing)$$

$$EBITDA = \$1,000,000 - (\$400,000 + \$100,000 + \$50,000)$$

$$EBITDA = \mathbf{\$450,000}$$

This figure represents the core profitability of the business, giving you a clear snapshot of how your brokerage is performing.

Conclusion

EBITDA is a critical metric for mortgage brokers because it strips away the noise and focuses on what matters – core operational profitability. It's a tool every broker should use to keep their business on track and grow steadily.

By understanding your EBITDA, you can benchmark your performance, manage debt, attract investment and ensure your business remains liquid and healthy. By focusing on EBITDA, you're not just looking at today's profits you're planning for tomorrow's success.

CHAPTER 23

Full valuation of your brokerage: The power of EBITDA in business sales

Many mortgage brokers are leaving value on the table when they focus solely on selling their trail books. The real power lies in understanding and leveraging EBITDA as a key driver in determining the true value of your mortgage broking business.

If you're planning to sell your business, it's crucial to consider the operational performance of the brokerage and not just the income generated by your trail book.

While 90% of sales in the industry focus on trail book sales, this approach fails to capture the full operational and financial value of a brokerage. It is not just the qualitative analysis of the trail book we went through before. It is a future-looking strategy made up of other overlooked elements such as current revenue streams from new clients you brought in, operational efficiency in hours, cost management in dollars, staff productivity and ability to bring in new business and growth opportunities going ahead.

Let's explore how mortgage brokers can enhance their business value through an EBITDA-centric sale strategy.

Why sell based on EBITDA instead of trail book value?

EBITDA provides a more comprehensive view of your brokerage's profitability by including core earnings and excluding non-operating expenses like interest and taxes. When selling your brokerage, EBITDA highlights operational performance and efficiency, allowing for a more accurate valuation and broader buyer interest.

Valuation advantage

EBITDA accounts for both operating profits and cost efficiencies, offering a fuller picture than simple trail book sales.

Businesses using EBITDA for valuation generally attract higher multiples. Small businesses might achieve one to three times EBITDA, while medium-sized firms can secure four to six times EBITDA.

Attracts savvy buyers

Buyers interested in a business beyond just its trail book (like private equity investors) often look for EBITDA figures. This opens up opportunities for higher-value transactions including buyouts of mature businesses.

Facilitates financing

Lenders prefer EBITDA as a measure of business health, making it easier for buyers to secure financing based on actual operational performance.

Steps to prepare your brokerage for an EBITDA sale

1. Review your financials

Start by conducting a detailed review of your profit and loss statements and balance sheet. Ensure that your records are organised and easy to understand.

Use industry benchmarking tools to compare your business performance with peers, which provides transparency and validates your business valuation.

2. Optimise operations for efficiency

Before putting your brokerage on the market, make sure it's operating efficiently:

Leverage technology: Automate repetitive tasks and use CRM tools to streamline lead management.

Diversify income streams: Go beyond residential loans and explore **asset finance**, **commercial loans** or **insurance referrals**.

Reduce unnecessary costs: Review your expenses, outsourcing where needed to improve margins.

Build a strong team: Ensure your staff is well-trained and can keep the business running smoothly during the transition.

3. Due diligence preparation

Gather all relevant documents for potential buyers, such as:

- tax returns and financial statements
- business assets, leases and liabilities
- employee records, contracts and referral agreements
- legal documents, like shareholders' agreements and business licences

- documented processes for operations, client engagement and compliance.

Having these organised will speed up the due diligence process and give buyers confidence in the professionalism and readiness of your business.

4. Professional valuation

Obtaining a professional valuation based on EBITDA is crucial. A business broker with experience in the mortgage broking industry can guide you on pricing, negotiation strategies and market conditions. Remember, your business is often undervalued if only trail book figures are considered.

5. Finalise legal agreements

Once a sale agreement is in place, work closely with legal advisors to ensure that the terms are airtight. Pay special attention to transition details, earn-out provisions (if applicable) and any warranties tied to the sale. Legal advice is critical here. You don't want to cut corners on this stage of the deal.

Enhancing EBITDA: Tips for maximising business value

To maximise the value of your brokerage based on EBITDA, consider these strategies:

- **Streamline operations**: Eliminate inefficiencies and automate processes where possible.
- **Focus on cost management**: Keep a close eye on unnecessary spending while improving service delivery.
- **Diversify income streams**: Broaden your revenue base beyond traditional mortgage products.
- **Invest in marketing and branding**: A stronger brand presence will attract better buyers and lead to higher valuations.

Conclusion

Selling your brokerage based on EBITDA opens up more opportunities for higher returns, bringing the operational performance of your business into the equation, not just its recurring income from trail books. By preparing your business for an EBITDA-focused sale you attract savvy buyers, including private equity investors, and position yourself for a higher valuation.

Ensure that your brokerage's operational efficiency, diverse income streams and technological infrastructure are optimised before considering a sale. This approach will lead to better offers and provide the financial flexibility to transition into your next phase, whether that's reinvesting in a new venture or enjoying a comfortable retirement.

Remember: Selling your business based on EBITDA and not just trail book value is the key to unlocking its full worth.

CHAPTER 24

Paying yourself as a mortgage broker: Navigating pre-drawings vs. post-drawings

When Andrew transitioned from being a top-performing employee at a major bank to a multi-award-winning mortgage broker, he thought he had everything under control. Even with years of accounting experience under his belt, there was one thing he hadn't anticipated – how to pay himself. He would dip into the business account whenever he needed personal funds, thinking, *It's my business. I'll just take money from there whenever I want.*

As months passed, Andrew noticed that cash flow was becoming tight, especially during slower periods.

His accountant warned him about his random withdrawals. These pre-drawings were affecting his business's ability to reinvest in growth. Worse, tax time was a mess. Andrew had failed to set aside enough for taxes, leading to a hefty and unexpected Division 293 bill from the ATO. Andrew is now on a payment plan with the ATO.

After consulting with our Profit team and getting a second opinion, Andrew has now revamped how he handled his business finances. He has started paying himself based on profit (after ensuring that expenses, tax and reinvestment goals are met), and this shift has given him the peace of mind that was lacking.

One of the most important aspects of successfully running your mortgage brokerage is deciding how you, as the business owner, pay yourself. Should you take money out before profit is calculated (pre-drawings) or after (post-drawings)? It's a question that trips up many brokers, especially when transitioning from being an employee to running their own brokerage.

The answer depends on your business structure, your financial goals and what's most tax-efficient for you. There is no one-size-fits-all, as it is more about you than the business. You do have to cover your personal expenses and live comfortably too.

Let's break this down in a way that's simple for both new and seasoned brokers exploring the pros and cons of each method while adding value through insights into long-term planning and tax efficiency.

Pre-drawings vs. post-drawings: What's the difference?

Pre-drawings refers to taking money out of your business before profit is officially calculated. It's essentially drawing from your business cash flow to meet personal needs. **Post-drawings**, on the other hand, involves waiting until after profits are calculated, ensuring you have a clear picture of the financial health of your brokerage before taking out any money.

Factors to consider

There are several critical factors to keep in mind when deciding between pre-drawings and post-drawings:

Tax bracket: Your personal tax bracket impacts whether it's more efficient to draw before or after profits.

Business structure: Whether you're a sole trader, partnership, company or family trust can significantly affect the implications of each option.

Financial goals: Are you focused on personal cash flow, or do you want to reinvest more into the business for growth?

Professional advice: Always consult with an accountant for specific advice related to your situation. This guide is educational and only provides general advice.

How to pay yourself as a mortgage broker based on your business structure

1. Sole trader

Pre-drawings earnings:

Flexibility: As a sole trader, you have flexibility in how and when you draw money. This can help with managing personal cash flow, as you're able to take funds when needed.

Tax implications: Your income tax is based on your net business income, so pre-drawings won't directly affect your tax obligations.

Budgeting: It's important to ensure you leave enough in the business to meet operating costs and tax obligations.

Post-drawings earnings:

Clarity: Taking money out after calculating profit gives you a clearer picture of the business's financial health.

Tax Planning: Post-drawings can help with more accurate tax planning, ensuring that you have set aside enough for taxes.

Reinvestment: You're prioritising the business by reinvesting profits, which can help grow the business faster.

2. Partnership

Pre-drawings earnings:

Partnership agreements: Drawing money before profit is calculated requires a clear agreement between partners on how much each can take.

Shared tax: Tax is shared based on the net income, regardless of how much each partner draws individually.

Post-drawings earnings:

Profit-based drawings: Partners typically draw earnings after profit is calculated and distributed according to the partnership agreement.

Reinvestment decisions: Profits can be reinvested collectively to grow the business.

Tax planning: This provides clarity for both partners when it comes to handling tax obligations.

3. Company

Pre-drawings earnings:

Director loans: If you take pre-drawings in a company structure, it's often treated as a director's loan – meaning, the business lends you money.

Complex tax implications: If you don't pay back the loan within the financial year, it may lead to tax complications.

Legalities: The Corporations Act 2001 regulates director's loans, so it's important to understand the legal boundaries.

Post-drawings earnings:

Dividends: Most profits in a company are drawn as dividends after taxes are calculated.

Clarity: This method provides a clear separation between personal and business finances.

Tax planning: Post-drawings facilitate better tax planning and ensure you are setting aside enough profit for future reinvestment.

4. Family trust

Pre-drawings earnings:

No pre-drawings: In a family trust structure, beneficiaries don't take pre-drawings. Distributions are made after profit is calculated.

Tax: Distributions are taxed at the individual beneficiaries' marginal tax rates.

Post-drawings earnings:

Tax flexibility: Trusts can distribute profits in a tax-effective manner to various beneficiaries, often taking advantage of income splitting.

Reinvestment: Trustees can decide to reinvest the profits back into the business if desired.

When should you take pre-drawings vs. post-drawings?

New brokers

When you're starting out, it's common not to take a salary immediately, but when you do, the post-drawings method might be the most sensible. It provides a clear picture of how well your business is doing before taking money out. This also allows you to **reinvest** as much as possible in the early stages, which is key for growth.

Established brokers

Bigger brokerages, especially those under family trust structures, often use post-drawings for tax efficiency. By waiting until after profit is calculated, they can distribute income to family members at lower tax brackets, reducing the overall tax burden. This strategy benefits long-term financial planning and ensures the business remains profitable.

Key takeaways

- **New brokers** should lean toward post-drawings to get a clear picture of their profits and allow for reinvestment.

- **Established brokers** in larger firms may benefit from family trust structures for more tax-effective income distribution.

- Always **consult your accountant** to ensure you're following the best approach for your personal and business financial health.

Conclusion

In the end, paying yourself is not just about taking money out of the business, it's about ensuring that your method aligns with your growth objectives, tax obligations and long-term success.

There is no one-size-fits-all answer when deciding how to pay yourself as a self-employed mortgage broker. Review it as you grow, as it will change over time as life happens and you restructure your business.

Whether you choose pre-drawings or post-drawings depends on factors such as your business structure, cash flow needs and long-term goals. What's most important is ensuring that whatever method you choose aligns with your financial goals and is tax-efficient.

Speak to your accountant and tax professional for personalised advice. The money you spend on sound accounting advice is invaluable.

CHAPTER 25

Maximising tax benefits for mortgage brokers: Navigating small business concessions

The end of the year often brings reflections for mortgage brokers, particularly those who have been in the industry for 15 years or longer. Many of these brokers consider whether it's time to transition out and sell their trail book and face questions about how best to maximise financial outcomes. A crucial aspect of this decision-making process involves understanding and leveraging small business tax concessions available to Australian mortgage brokers.

Let's dive into four major tax concessions every broker should understand, whether they are planning to sell their business soon or simply thinking ahead. But remember these concessions are complex and should be discussed with a qualified accountant for personalised advice.

1) The 15-year exemption: The ultimate retirement bonus

If you are a mortgage broker aged 55 or over, retiring or facing permanent incapacity and have owned your business for at least 15 years, you could be eligible for a full exemption from **capital gains tax (CGT)** when selling your business. This allows you to retain all profits from the sale without paying tax on them.

Case study: Icon's retirement

Icon, a 70-year-old broker with 30 years of business under his belt, decides it's time to retire. With the 15-year exemption, Icon sells his well-established brokerage, and all profits from the sale are completely exempt from CGT. This translates to significant tax savings, providing Icon with financial freedom to enjoy retirement.

2) The 50% active asset reduction: Boosting your sale profits

When selling an asset actively used in your business, such as your client database or office space, the 50% active asset reduction can halve your capital gain. This reduction works in conjunction with the general CGT discount, which further reduces the capital gain by another 50% if you've held the asset for over a year. For brokers, this could mean a 75% reduction in capital gains tax!

Case study: Cera's office space sale

Cera, a broker in Melbourne, sells her office after running her business from the space for more than 10 years. By applying both the 50% active asset reduction and the general CGT discount, Cera effectively reduces her tax liability on the sale, keeping more of her profits.

3) The retirement exemption: A lifeline for super contributions

This concession allows you to exempt up to $500,000 of the capital gain from tax if you sell an active business asset. If you're under 55, you'll need to reinvest the exempted amount into a complying superannuation fund, making it a great tool for boosting retirement savings. This exemption is a lifetime limit; meaning, that over the course of your career, you can utilise it up to $500,000 in total.

Case study: Alessandro's partial sale

At 48, Alessandro decides to sell a portion of his trail book to fund personal expenses. The sale generates a significant profit, and Alessandro is able to exempt up to $500,000 of the capital gain by using the retirement exemption. Since he's under 55, Alessandro invests the exempted amount into his superfund, giving his retirement savings a significant boost while enjoying a tax break.

4) Rollover relief: Deferring capital gains

When you sell a business or asset and reinvest in another business asset, rollover relief allows you to defer capital gains tax until you sell the newly acquired asset. This is especially beneficial for brokers expanding their businesses or restructuring their assets without facing immediate tax obligations.

Case study: Bel's expansion

Bel, a broker, sells her current office premises and reinvests the proceeds in a larger property to support her growing team. By utilising rollover relief, Bel defers paying CGT on the sale, preserving her cash flow for business expansion. This allows her to focus on growth without an immediate tax burden.

Important considerations

Eligibility:
To qualify for these concessions, you'll need to meet specific criteria set by the ATO. This includes details like how long you've held an asset and whether it's classified as an active business asset.

Business structure:
Whether you operate as a sole trader, partnership or under a trust structure can influence how you apply these tax concessions. Always review this with a professional.

The ATO's scrutiny:
The ATO will examine how you used these assets – whether for business or personal purposes – and your broader business structure when assessing your eligibility for these benefits.

Action steps

1. Consult your accountant to see which tax concessions apply to your situation.
2. If you're planning to sell your business or assets, ensure you meet all criteria for the relevant concessions.

3. Explore whether reinvestment through roll-over relief could be a smart move for your business expansion.

Conclusion

For mortgage brokers considering selling their business, these small business tax concessions can lead to substantial savings. By understanding the options available and planning ahead, you can ensure a smooth transition while maximising your financial return.

These tax benefits can give mortgage brokers the financial cushion they need to retire comfortably or reinvest for growth. Whether it's the 15-year exemption, the 50% active asset reduction or the roll-over relief, these concessions offer powerful tools for retirement planning and business growth.

CHAPTER 26

Bucket company strategies: The smart tax move for mortgage brokers

Ever wondered how top mortgage brokers manage to keep more of their hard-earned profits? One of the clever strategies they use is setting up bucket companies. While this may sound a bit technical, it's actually a great way to minimise taxes, protect assets and reinvest in your business.

Rivka, a former accountant, had built her 20-year-old business as she provided excellent service to clients from her local synagogue and tight-knit community. Balancing her business and family life as a mother of three, Rivka had personal expenses to manage.

Her admin staff, who had been with her for 10 years, wanted to become a broker. Rivka felt trapped by the constant tug of wanting to expand her broker team, hire more admin staff while not losing a massive chunk of income to taxes.

We advised her that by setting up a bucket company, Rivka could distribute her profits to the company. Instead of taking all her profits directly into her personal account, she could store a significant portion in the bucket company, freeing up more cash for business reinvestment. They'd be taxed at a flat rate of 30%, far less than the 45% personal income tax she was currently paying. This structure would protect her profits from any legal risks that might arise from running a business.

By the end of the last financial year, Rivka's business had transformed, thanks to her cousin and also her accountant setting up the strategy. She had saved over $50,000 in tax money and used it to hire two new brokers. With her expanded team, Rivka was able to serve more clients and give back to her community, donating generously to her synagogue and local charities. The bucket company had not only allowed her to grow her brokerage and fulfil her commitment to tithing.

Even if you're a new broker, understanding the basics of this strategy can help you structure your business in a way that sets you up for long-term success.

Let's break down the benefits of a bucket company strategy in simple terms so you can see how it might work for your broking business.

1. Keep more of what you earn

Nobody likes paying more tax than they have to, right? One of the main advantages of using a bucket company is the ability to distribute your profits to a company that may be taxed at a lower rate than an individual.

Let's say your trust earns a profit of $200,000. If you distribute that to yourself (and you're in a high tax bracket), you could be paying up to 45% tax. That's $90,000 in tax! However, if you distribute it to your bucket company, which has a flat tax rate of 30%, you'll only pay $60,000, saving you $30,000. Pretty good, right?

2. Shield your profits from risk

Running a broking business involves risk, especially with compliance and client satisfaction. Profits transferred to a bucket company are protected from personal creditors, which is essential if a professional lawsuit or legal claim ever comes your way.

If you have a compliance issue and you have a legal claim against you, a personal liability for your profits would expose your profits to creditors. However, the funds do have some protection if it is kept in your bucket company.

3. Use some of your profits to reinvest in your business.

The cash you retain in a bucket company can be more than just parked for the future. You can use it to reinvest in your business today. Whether that be more staff, new technology or new marketing campaigns, it's a clever way to ensure your profits remain working for you.

Let's assume that your bucket company has been able to build up $500,000 over five years. This is the money you can use to hire new brokers, create a more robust marketing team or even expand into new services. Pumping back in will allow your business to grow further without requiring external financing.

4. Paying yourself the smart way

One of the cool things about a bucket company is that it can distribute dividends to shareholders, which often come with franking (or imputation) credits. This helps prevent double taxation and can reduce your personal tax bill.

For instance, if your bucket company distributes a $70,000 dividend to you, and it carries a franking credit of $30,000 (representing the tax already paid by the company), you can use that credit to reduce your personal tax liability. It's a win-win.

5. Smooth transition

Planning for the future? A trust used in combination with a bucket company can make it easier to transfer assets without triggering significant tax or stamp duty liabilities. This is especially handy if you're planning to pass your business onto a partner or family member.

Let's say, a senior broker nearing retirement might want to transfer the business to a spouse or child. By using a bucket company and trust structure, they can do this without incurring massive tax bills. It's a great way to ensure a smooth transition and protect your legacy.

6. Income Splitting (my favourite trick!)

This is where it gets fun – income splitting. This way, you avoid everybody **involved** being hit with a sore tax bill by allocating the profits to various family members and/or to the bucket company.

Let's say you manage the Rich Family Trust, with $2 million in profits. In reality, without income splitting, if you gave all that to Mr Rich, who is already earning $1 million, his tax would be through the roof. Rather, give $250,000 to Mr Rich (below top tax bracket), $250,000 to Mrs Rich (part-time employee with lower income), $50,000 to their 18-year-old daughter (who works in a laundromat) and the final $1.45m to the bucket company (taxable at a flat rate). Smart, right?

Things to think about: Set-up and operational expenses

There are also costs involved in setting up a bucket company, both time and moneywise. You'll have to monitor compliance and legalities, and check that all is structured properly. **With every passing year,** the ATO is **getting more and more** vigilant for suspected tax avoidance schemes. It's crucial that you engage a competent accountant to implement this strategy.

Conclusion

Bucket companies can provide mortgage brokers with amazing benefits, from tax savings to business growth potential, but they aren't a one-size-fits-all solution. The wisdom is in finding the right professional guidance and ensuring your strategy is in line with your business objectives.

If you're just starting out, or if you already have a successful brokerage, they might be just what you need to build wealth and future-proof your business. So, how are you going to take the plunge? Contact your tax accountant and discover your options.

CHAPTER 27

Boosting profits: Smart strategies for mortgage brokers to maximise operating income

As mortgage brokers, we work hard to make property dreams a reality for our clients, but generating great revenue doesn't always mean we're maximising profits. With rising competition and increasing operational demands, brokers must find smart ways to boost their bottom line while also keeping clients happy.

Here are some fun, easy-to-understand strategies that will help you increase your operating profits without adding unnecessary stress to your business.

1. 'Would you like fries with that?'

We all know the power of the McDonald's famous upsell – 'Would you like fries with that?'. This simple question has boosted their revenue for decades, and it's time brokers start thinking like McDonald's. Why stick to just residential loans? Expanding into asset finance, commercial loans and even insurance referrals can significantly increase your average revenue per client without extra heavy lifting.

You don't even have to handle these deals yourself! Many aggregators now have internal referral hubs where you can pass on commercial or asset finance leads and earn a commission. This not only increases revenue but also positions you as a one-stop shop for your clients' financial needs.

2. Work smarter, not harder

Let's face it, technology is your friend. If you're still doing everything manually, you're missing out on tools that could save you hours of work each week. Use CRM systems to streamline client management, set up digital document storage to keep things organised, and automate emails, updates and signing paperwork with tools like HubSpot and Docusign respectively. It's about working smarter, not harder.

Tools to explore:
- **Fathom** to benchmark and set financial goals.
- **Google Drive** or **OneDrive** for seamless document storage.
- **Tableau** or **Google Data Studio** for easy data analysis and client reporting.

By automating repetitive tasks, you free up more time to focus on building relationships and winning new business

3. Happy clients, bigger profits

Happy clients are your best form of marketing. In fact, it costs five times more to attract a new client than to keep an existing one.

Implement regular post-settlement check-ins, send clients market updates and don't be afraid to run referral competitions to get them talking about your services. Every client you retain and every referral you receive means more profit with less effort.

4. Knowledge is power

Your business will only grow as much as you do. In today's digital age, learning is easier (and cheaper)

than ever. Platforms like YouTube, LinkedIn Learning and podcasts make world-class business and personal development content accessible at your fingertips. You can learn from industry leaders like Tony Robbins or business experts like Alex Hormozi without having to leave your office.

Tip: Make it a habit to watch or listen to one piece of self-development content every week. The insights you gain will have a ripple effect on how you run your business and interact with clients.

---

5. Every dollar counts

Take a closer look at where your money is going and cut unnecessary overhead. This might mean moving to a coworking space instead of leasing a full office or outsourcing non-core tasks like admin or marketing. Every dollar you save is an extra dollar in your pocket – money that can be used to invest in your business or increase your take-home pay.

By switching from a high-rent office space to a flexible coworking arrangement, brokers can save thousands annually. These savings can be redirected to marketing efforts or employee training to grow your business faster.

6. Leverage social media and content

Traditional advertising is no longer the only way to market yourself. With social media platforms like TikTok, Instagram and LinkedIn, mortgage brokers can reach new clients without spending big bucks. Creating short, informative videos about mortgage tips or client success stories can go viral and introduce you to a younger, digital-savvy audience. Plus, content marketing like blogs and newsletters keeps you on top of clients' minds.

Tip: Engage with your community by sponsoring local events, attending networking groups or supporting local charities. This builds trust and helps you stand out in a crowded market.

7. Expand your referral network

Think beyond the typical real estate agents and accountants, and build partnerships with local businesses that complement your services. This includes commercial builders, conveyancers, financial planners and even home stagers. By collaborating with a wider range of partners, you create a stronger referral network that brings in more consistent business.

For instance, partnering with car dealerships for vehicle loans or property developers for new homes can open doors to new client opportunities and build a steady stream of referrals. These possibilities with such collaborators include and aren't limited to:

- commercial builders
- asset finance
- insurance agents
- real estate agents
- accountants
- wills and estate planning lawyers
- conveyancers and buyer's advocates
- car dealerships
- financial planners
- property developers
- local community
- sporting clubs
- chamber of commerce
- Business Network International (BNI) or other networking groups
- credit agencies
- home inspectors and appraisers
- home stagers or interior decorators
- movers and removalists

Conclusion

Running a successful mortgage broking business in today's competitive market requires a blend of traditional and innovative strategies. By embracing technology, expanding your services and building strong community ties, you can boost your operating profits while also keeping your clients happy.

In the end, it's about working smarter, providing value and daring to do things a little differently. So, open up Google or use AI to locate all the collaborators listed above that are close to you. Pick up the phone and call them or book a time to meet with them with the intention of being of service and picking up business from them along the way.

CHAPTER 28

Lessons from Ryanair: How mortgage brokers can grow profits

Mortgage brokers often ask whether being a solo operator or running a large brokerage leads to greater profitability. It's a valid question, and we can learn a lot from the aviation industry, particularly from Ryanair – Europe's largest low-cost airline.

A lot of brokers look at the billion-dollar brokers and think they cannot get there. They make excuses that billion-dollar brokers have big teams, started at a better time or have more money to advertise and build their brands. They give up even before putting in a good fight.

All that shines is not gold. Whilst the top brokers are winning the awards and writing massive volumes, are they truly profitable? Is the take-home money post-expenses and growing of staff better than yours when you pro rata it?

For context, Ryanair, with its no-frills approach, outperformed the globally renowned Emirates in terms of profitability in 2022, 2023 and 2024! Ryanair made a profit of US$1.4 billion in 2022, whilst Emirates made US$296 million. In 2024, Ryanair's profit margin was 15.3% against Emirates's 14.2%.

So, why is Ryanair so successful? And even more crucially, how can mortgage brokers implement these lessons to expand their businesses?

Lean and simple cost leadership

Ryanair's approach:
Ryanair keeps its operational costs down by relying on secondary airports, flying one type of aircraft and scrapping unnecessary services. This simplicity in its operations allows for lower prices to customers, enabling it to be competitive without sacrificing profit margins.

For mortgage brokers:

Mortgage brokers can take a similar approach by making operations more efficient. Such standardisation can be in the form of a uniform process, automation or a structured way of using a single CRM that integrates all the tools at one point, bringing down time and resources. Cutting costs where possible (working from coworking spaces rather than renting large offices, for example) helps you get this cost passed onto clients at a more affordable price (or reinvested into the business).

Another example is brokers who invest in an aggregator like Quickli (which holds all servicing calculators) are able to streamline their client service processes. This cuts down on the time spent going back and forth, making it easier to respond promptly, similar to Ryanair's fast turnaround times for flights.

Focus on simplified offerings

Ryanair's approach:

Ryanair is a no-frills carrier and will sell you a seat and little else. Customers can pay additional fees for add-ons such as seat selection or checking in baggage.

For mortgage brokers:

Similarly, mortgage brokers can simplify their product range. Instead of servicing every loan product under the sun, brokers can specialise in niches, like first home buyer (FHB) loans, commercial loans or investment loans. Keep your product limited to only the things you know well, narrow down what you sell and hone in on expertise with what you provide.

Fewer choices lead to less decision fatigue for your clients, so narrowing your offerings to people with whom you want to work can make the mortgage process easier and quicker. This 'focused expertise' approach can also increase your efficiency, enabling you to deal with more loans in less time, much like Ryanair operates a greater number of flights per day by concentrating on shorter and simpler routes.

Ancillary revenue streams

Ryanair's approach:

Ryanair earns a large percentage of its revenue through ancillary services, such as baggage fees and in-flight purchases. This add-on charge model enables the airline to offer low base fares while remaining profitable.

For mortgage brokers:

Brokers can drive profit growth by providing extra products and services on top of the core mortgage broking, similar to Ryanair. Consider offering ancillary services such as personal loans, asset finance, home insurance or business loans. Adding these services increases your value to clients as well as diversifies your income streams, which will shield you from any dips in the property market.

Similarly, brokers can generate additional revenue streams (much as Ryanair does with its add-ons) by directing customers to trusted partners to purchase insurance or additional financial services.

Focus on providing effective customer service

Ryanair's approach:
Ryanair is (relatively) a budget airline and has invested in improving customer service over the years to ensure repeat business and brand loyalty.

For mortgage brokers:
A good level of customer service doesn't have to cost a mortgage broker a fortune. Automated email updates on loan status, personalised advice and regular check-ins to discuss repricing opportunities are just a few ways to keep your clients happy. These small touches can make a significant difference in client retention and referrals.

Consistently following up with your clients post-settlement or helping them renegotiate their rates every six months can turn satisfied clients into repeat customers. Just like with Ryanair benefitting from loyal customers booking again, satisfied clients in broking can bring in referrals that lead to higher, long-term profitability.

Conclusion

Ryanair's model based on simplicity, cost-efficiency, ancillary revenue and consistent customer service holds valuable lessons for mortgage brokers – the size of your business doesn't necessarily determine profitability. Whether you're a one-person operation or managing a larger brokerage, efficiency, smart revenue streams and excellent service will drive your business forward.

The mortgage industry is filled with challenges, but using the right strategies can lead to consistent profitability no matter your size. By focusing on cost management, streamlining operations and looking for new ways to serve your clients, you can grow your brokerage much like Ryanair has grown to become a leading force in its industry.

Recap of Section 3: Mastering financial health

Chapter 20: Brokerage's finances: A simple and strategic chart of accounts

- Separate upfront commissions (residential, commercial and asset finance), trail commissions and referral revenue to easily track earnings.

- Track aggregator fees, commission splits and clawbacks in your COGS to monitor deal profitability

- Ensure accurate expense classification and expected taxes, and lodge your BAS in time.

Chapter 21: Prioritising net profit over gross revenue

- Track net profit, factoring in all expenses to provide a clearer financial snapshot.

- Reduce unnecessary overhead costs such as office space, client gifts, printing or travel to increase your profit margins.

- Compare your brokerage's profitability with local peers.

Chapter 22: Mastering EBITDA

- Track EBITDA to measure operational profitability.

- Benchmark against peers focusing on cost-efficiency and profitability.

- Ensure your EBITDA allows for growth expenditures without financial strain.

Chapter 23: Full valuation of your brokerage using EBITDA

- Prepare for an EBITDA sale to present your brokerage as an operationally profitable business.

- Improve your EBITDA by reducing costs, increasing efficiency and diversifying income streams.

- Get a professional valuation rather than solely focusing on trail book value.

Chapter 24: Paying yourself: Pre-drawings vs. post-drawings

- Consult an accountant on the most tax-efficient way to pay yourself depending on your business structure.

- Wait until profits are calculated before paying yourself to gain clarity on business financial health and ensure reinvestment in growth.

- Establish a consistent pay structure to ensure tax compliance and cash flow for both your personal and business needs.

Chapter 25: Maximising tax benefits and small business concessions

- Explore the 15-year exemption if you are nearing retirement and have owned your business for over 15 years.

- Utilise the 50% active asset reduction to reduce the capital gains tax on business assets, like your client database or office space.

- Reinforce your retirement strategy using the retirement exemption or rollover relief to optimise tax savings.

Chapter 26: Bucket company strategies

- Work with an accountant to establish a bucket company for tax savings.

- Distribute profits between family members to lower the tax burden across lower-income brackets.

- Reinvest tax savings by hiring staff, upgrading technology or expanding services.

Chapter 27: Boosting profits and maximising operating income

- Introduce services like asset finance, commercial loans and insurance referrals to increase revenue per client.

- Leverage technology to streamline operations and increase efficiency.

- Implement post-settlement check-ins and client referral programs to increase repeat business.

Chapter 28: Lessons from Ryanair on growing profits

- Simplify brokerage processes and reduce operational costs by using technology and workflows.

- Offer additional financial services to be a one-stop financial shop.

- Improve client experience (CX) through auto-mated updates, personalised communications and proactive loan repricing reviews.

CHAPTER 29

Scaling smart: When and how to add staff to your mortgage brokerage

Ethan, a mortgage broker based in South Australia, had always been a self-starter. After leaving a job at one of the four major banks, he launched his own brokerage with a handful of loyal clients in Australia's seafood capital city. Word-of-mouth referrals started pouring in thanks to his face-to-face old-fashioned service.

Within two years, Ethan was consistently closing $4 million in loans each month, but he was also working 14-hour days with no weekends. He was juggling everything from client meetings to paperwork and compliance. His phone rang constantly, and his email inbox overflowed. Ethan has a young family and missed important family events. He found himself barely keeping up with the growing demands of his business. Ethan's ability to manage everything alone was unsustainable, leaving it to the last minute.

One day, Ethan realised something had to change after he nearly lost a key client because he couldn't respond quickly enough. Word spreads quickly in small towns, and he could not afford the negative press. Working in his business and training new staff means his finances would take a hit for the next couple of years.

As a self-employed mortgage broker, deciding when to hire more staff is a critical step towards growing your business and maintaining balance in your life. The goal is to scale strategically, ensuring that the business grows efficiently without overextending your financial resources or jeopardising the quality of your service.

This chapter will guide you through recognising the right time to bring in new team members – whether you're hiring support staff, brokers or an operations manager.

The misconception of hiring early

One common piece of advice is to **hire as early as possible** so you're always resourced for growth. While this might work for some, it can be financially and operationally risky for others, especially if you haven't budgeted or planned for the added costs. Instead, you need to ensure that your business revenue and workload support the decision to hire while recognising that new staff will require training, management and mentorship and may not have the same level of commitment you do as the business owner.

When to hire a new broker?

Bringing on an additional broker can relieve you of client-facing pressures and help you expand your offerings. Here are some clear signs that it's time to add another broker to your team:

High volume of leads and settlement: If you're consistently settling between $2 million and $5 million a month and are unable to handle the growing volume of leads, it's a strong indicator that you need another broker.

New brokers require training and will expect mentorship. You need to ensure that you have the bandwidth to guide them and the right processes in place to onboard them efficiently.

Diversify your loan offerings: If clients are asking for loan types you don't specialise in, such as commercial loans, asset finance or personal loans, hiring a specialist in these areas can help you capture new revenue streams and serve your clients better.

Work–life imbalance: If you're consistently working over 50 to 60 hours a week with no weekends in sight, you need to start thinking about delegation before you burn out.

When to hire an operations manager?

An operations manager is essential once your business grows beyond what you can personally handle. Their role will encompass daily operations, managing staff, overseeing payroll and ensuring everything runs smoothly in your absence. Hiring an operations manager frees up your time to focus on big-picture strategy rather than being bogged down by the nitty-gritty of running the business. Here's when you should consider adding one:

Having a considerable team size and revenue: If you're managing a team of more than three or four people, and your annual revenue exceeds $2 million, you're likely spending too much time on the day-to-day operations, which an operations manager can handle while you focus on growing the business.

Plans for growth and scale: If you have aggressive growth plans, such as expanding into new markets or significantly increasing the size of your team, an operations manager will be essential to laying the groundwork.

When to hire support staff (onshore/offshore)?

Support staff handle the bulk of the administrative work, including tasks like coordinating appointments, preparing loan documents and managing your CRM. allowing you to focus on high-value tasks such as closing deals and building relationships. Here's how to know if it's time to hire:

Administrative burden: If more than 40 to 50% of your day is spent on administrative tasks – such as managing documents, following up with clients, handling emails and chasing lenders – it's time to bring on support staff.

Steady revenue: A good rule of thumb is to ensure your business is bringing in regular monthly revenue between $15,000 and $25,000. This way, you can sustain the additional salary, superannuation, bonuses and other perks (like leave and amenities) that come with hiring support staff.

Pro Tip: Offshore support staff can be a more cost-effective option for tasks that don't require onshore presence, allowing you to reduce expenses without sacrificing quality.

Key considerations before hiring

Cash flow analysis
Before you make any hiring decisions, ensure that you've done a thorough cash flow analysis. Bringing on new staff should help grow the business, not strain its resources.

Job descriptions
Write up detailed job descriptions that define the roles and responsibilities of each hire. This ensures clarity and helps you measure their performance against your business goals.

Strategic alignment
Make sure your hiring decisions align with your long-term business strategy. If you're only looking for temporary relief during a particularly busy season or personal leave, hiring a contractor or part-time staff might be a better solution.

Onboarding and training
Ensure you have documented processes in place to onboard and train new hires effectively. This is especially

important for new brokers who will be working under your licence, as any compliance issues could affect the future of your business.

Legal and HR considerations

Be aware of any employment law changes and the challenges that come with managing a larger team. For instance, a PAYG employee might require sick leave, annual leave or even maternity leave, which could create cash flow challenges for smaller businesses.

Actionable takeaways

1. **Hire brokers** when you can't handle the volume of leads or want to diversify your services.

2. **Bring in an operations manager** when you're spending more time managing the business than growing it.

3. **Hire support staff** when administrative tasks take up too much of your day, preventing you from focusing on high-value activities.

4. **Plan ahead** by doing a cash flow analysis and setting up clear processes for training and onboarding.

Conclusion

Expanding your team is a significant decision that should be made with both quantitative (revenue, settlements) and qualitative (workload, client care) factors in mind. While the right staff can help you scale faster, each hire should be strategic and align with both your current business needs and future growth plans.

With the right team in place, your brokerage will not only run more smoothly but also scale more efficiently, allowing you to focus on what matters most – growing your business. By following these guidelines, you'll be well on your way to building a robust and successful mortgage brokerage that can scale sustainably.

CHAPTER 30

Building a sales-driven culture: Essential selling skills across every role in your brokerage

In any small business, particularly in a mortgage brokerage, the line between roles can blur, especially when it comes to sales and customer service. Success isn't just determined by the head broker but by everyone from reception to the credit analyst. By ensuring all roles understand their impact on the sales process, brokers can grow their business and foster a culture of excellence that sets them apart.

Let's dive into how each role in your brokerage plays a key part in the sales process and what skills or strategies can be adopted to maximise these contributions.

The power of reception

The office manager or receptionist is often the first point of contact with clients. Their role is not just administrative; it's pivotal in setting the tone for the entire client experience. A warm, professional greeting can be the initial buy-in that makes clients feel comfortable and valued from the get-go.

How to do it right:

- **Training in customer service**: Equip your receptionist with a script that outlines key talking points, ensuring a welcoming and helpful demeanour with every interaction.
- **Professional presentation**: A tidy workspace, coupled with an inviting personality, enhances professionalism.
- **Initial engagement strategy**: Train receptionists to provide concise, helpful information and brochures or guides about your services when potential clients walk through the door. This ensures that, from the start, clients know they're dealing with experts.

The role of the client services manager

Client services go beyond paperwork. A well-managed account service can foster trust and loyalty, ensuring that clients stay long-term. The key is in the relationship-building aspect of this role. If done right, it can even lead to referrals.

How to do it right:
- **Active listening**: Training in empathetic and active listening helps client services managers better understand client concerns.
- **CRM mastery**: Mastering the CRM system ensures they can track every step of the client's journey, which aids in anticipating client needs.
- **Continuous updates**: Keeping clients updated on their loan process at each milestone reassures them and reduces anxiety.

Proactive communication: When a bottleneck arises, explaining what's happening and offering potential solutions can turn a frustrated client into a loyal one.

The credit analyst's unique advantage

A credit analyst can recommend options that go beyond the broker's usual go-to lenders. They have deep knowledge of the financial aspects of each loan, giving them a unique opportunity to provide solutions that not only meet but exceed client expectations.

How to do it right:
- **Lender interaction**: Ensure credit analysts regularly attend lender workshops or coffee clusters to stay informed on competitive products.
- **Product comparison**: Teach analysts to analyse multiple products and offer data-driven comparisons that clients will appreciate, helping them feel more confident in their decisions.
- **Scenario planning**: Use what-if scenarios to offer clients alternatives (Plan B options) such as different rates or terms they might not have considered but would work better for their financial goals.

The junior broker's role in growth

Junior brokers represent the future of your business. By harnessing their enthusiasm and giving them the right mentorship, they can handle client relations, ask for business and help alleviate the workload from the head broker.

How to do it right:

- **Structured mentorship**: Provide shadowing opportunities with experienced brokers and involve junior brokers in both client and partner meetings.
- **Documentation habits**: Teach them to record detailed notes on all client interactions, which enhances communication across the team.
- **Sales training**: Equip them with the skills to ask for business, how to handle objections and how to upsell services or additional products. This doesn't come naturally but can be taught.

The head broker's role

The head broker sets the tone for the entire business. They must demonstrate leadership by example, showcasing the values of discipline, service and accountability.

How to do it right:

- **Lead by example**: Show up with the same energy and commitment that you expect from your team. Share stories of success and failure, creating a learning environment.
- **Foster transparency**: Hold regular team meetings where everyone feels they have a stake in the business. When everyone knows

the brokerage's vision, they work with a clear purpose.

- **Continuous improvement culture**: Create a feedback loop where you share insights, strategies and client feedback regularly. This ensures that everyone in the team stays aligned and works towards improving service delivery.

Fostering a culture of excellence

In a small brokerage, it's not just about roles, it's about creating an environment where everyone understands their contribution to the business's success. By ensuring open communication channels, making continuous learning a priority and rewarding client success, brokers can create an atmosphere where everyone is emotionally invested in seeing the business succeed.

Recognition at every stage will further motivate the team to perform at their best, so footprints of everyone's work must be traceable – from the initial inquiry at reception to the final deal signed off by the head broker. When everyone feels connected to the outcomes, they'll naturally put in their best efforts to build something that lasts.

Conclusion

While individual selling skills vary by role, the essence of mortgage broking is creating an experience for the client that feels seamless, personalised and genuine. The more each member of the team invests in learning how to contribute to that experience, the more profitable and sustainable the brokerage becomes.

By following this approach, you can build not only a more efficient team but one that works together to drive long-term growth and client satisfaction. Each person in your brokerage has a part to play in selling, and when all parts work in harmony, the results can be transformative.

CHAPTER 31

Mastering mentorship for mortgage brokers: Unlocking your full potential

In the competitive world of mortgage broking, the significance of mentorship for brokers looking to grow and succeed can be substantial. If you are a fresher or already in the mortgage broking industry, a right mentor can propel your career, hone your skills and offer insights that could take years to gain.

Mentors are necessary at every level. Every top business owner has a mentor, regardless of where they are in their entrepreneurial journey. It is something you have to get right. Yet, many brokers still underestimate the importance of mentorship or fall into the trap of choosing a mentor that doesn't align with their specific needs.

Changing mentors costs you time and money that you don't have, especially when you are starting out. You need a mentor sign-off. Let's dive into the various mentorship opportunities available for mortgage brokers and how you can select the right one to unlock your full potential.

Why every mortgage broker should have a mentor

The reason why many brokers are reluctant to initiate mentorship stems from the age-old belief that experience is the best teacher. It can be a difficult framework to be trapped in. This could hold you back from developing and there are many errors that you may encounter, which can easily be averted with the right guidance.

A mentor will waive your learning curve, connect you with industry contacts, and suggest proven approaches and advice specific to your situation. However, not all mentorship programs are made equal, and selecting the right type can either break or make your career.

You hear of mentors who are fulltime mortgage brokers themselves and don't have the time to mentor you correctly. To get the best outcome, you need to find a mentor who is solely a mentor or a fulltime mentor who occasionally writes deals.

Types of mentorship programs available for mortgage brokers

1. Mentorships through industry bodies

Industry bodies such as the Finance Brokers Association of Australia (FBAA) and the Mortgage and Finance Association of Australia (MFAA) offer structured mentorship programs that connect new brokers with industry veterans and expose the newly minted associates to niche knowledge, best practice information and contractual compliance data.

> **Who it's for:** Brokers interested in structured education with a solid emphasis on compliance and industry standards.

> **Value added:** Helps establish credibility, looking to provide those relationships as essential.

2. Mentorship programs through franchise(s) or aggregators

Many of the leading aggregator groups provide in-house mentorships. These may include blueprints, online resources and peer networks geared around everything – from writing various loan types to taking care of yourself as a broker.

> **Who it's for:** Brokers seeking comprehensive, ongoing support, plus a step-by-step guide to growing a business.

> **Value added:** Existing home office lounge pants required, as it is a remote online program that provides you with access to videos, training and business models (mostly for brokers not their support staff).

3. Independent mentor services

Mentoring is provided by both private firms and experienced industry professionals (ex-aggregator directors, BDMs or successful brokers). These mentors are experts in individualised coaching that focuses on leadership, business strategy and scaling.

> **Who it's for:** Agents requiring customised, one-on-one coaching for personal and business growth.

Make sure that value-added providers focus on personalised growth and unlock revenue through personalised strategies.

4. Networking and informal mentorships

Informal mentorship can be found in local networking groups and online forums. Peer-to-peer learning can be priceless, particularly when it comes to understanding local market conditions or addressing everyday challenges.

Who it's for: Brokers looking for community-based learning.

Value added: Informal mentorship fosters lasting ties and provides practical, real-world insights from people who encounter the same problems as you.

5. Banks and lender-specific training

Lenders and banks provide product training, keeping brokers up to date on new offerings, lending criteria and compliance changes. These programs are essential for ensuring brokers offer the most accurate, up-to-date advice to clients.

Who it's for: Brokers focusing on product knowledge and lender relationships.

Value added: Equips you with specific knowledge to better serve clients and keep pace with industry changes.

6. Specialised business coaches

For brokers and business coaches, particularly those who specialise in the mortgage industry, who guide clients in setting goals, fine-tuning sales strategies and improving their bottom line. Many of these coaches are building scalable systems, creating efficiencies and scaling up referral partners.

Who it's for: Brokers who want to scale their business and build their teams.

Value added: These coaches aid in expanding a brokerage beyond just loan settlement numbers.

7. Sales training programs

Mentorship focused on sales can enhance your client interaction abilities, enhance conversion rates and train you how to plan your brokerage for advancement.

Who it's for: Business owners seeking to refine their sales strategies.

Value added: Offers effective tips for growing your active client lists and settlement volumes.

8. Mentors in digital marketing

As the mortgage industry embraces digitisation, brokers can cultivate an online presence and improve lead generation and branding with the help of a mentor focused on digital marketing.

Who it's for: Business owners seeking to make a strong digital footprint.

Value added: Aids in increasing your online visibility, enhancing your Google reviews and social media tactics.

Choosing the right mentor

When embarking on a mentorship, it's important to have clear expectations:

Goals: These are the specifics of what you want to accomplish.

Frequency of meeting: Come to an agreement on how often you will meet in person and virtually.

Mentorship duration: Hours and time frame of the mentorship.

Outcomes: Clearly define the outcomes you are aiming for at the conclusion of the mentorship.

Mentor fees: How much of your trail commissions do they feed on as monthly mentor fees? If your mentor is going to take 50% of your commissions, they better be processing all of your deals with you – from lodgement through to settlement – and giving you leads and desk space and all of that. It would be reasonable for you to pay 20% to 25% or a flat fee of about $500 per month, which is the industry standard.

By establishing these expectations up front, you will set yourself up, as well as your mentor, for success so you can make the most of the value the mentorship has to offer.

However, always keep in mind to ask for the testimonials or case studies of their previous customers before hiring a mentor. This can give you insights as to how they work as well as if their style suits your needs.

Conclusion

While mentorship is not a must, it helps significantly in your journey of becoming the best mortgage broker. The right mentorship program can accelerate your growth, help you avoid costly mistakes and build a more sustainable venture.

If you need help with compliance, business strategy, sales training or digital marketing, there is a mentor for you. With a clear understanding of expectations and a solid fit, mentorship will take your brokerage to the next level.

CHAPTER 32

Tailored commission splits and support models for retaining mortgage brokers

In every thriving mortgage brokerage, head brokers are constantly on the lookout for the right commission split that motivates brokers while ensuring retention. It's no secret that once a broker grows in experience and starts generating solid business, the thought of going independent often crosses their mind. The challenge, then, becomes 'What commission split and level of back-office support will keep brokers loyal while allowing the head broker to step back from day-to-day operations?'.

This chapter delves into the different support models that can be offered to brokers and the corresponding commission splits. By aligning the support provided with the split structure, head brokers can ensure both the profitability of the business and the long-term retention of brokers.

Let's break it down into three practical models.

Model 1: Fulltime back-office support (38 hours)

Suggested commission split:
70/30 in favour of the head broker

For brokers who require comprehensive end-to-end support, a commission split heavily favouring the head broker makes sense. Full-time back-office support takes care of the majority of the administrative and processing workload, allowing brokers to focus solely on client acquisition and relationship-building.

What does full support look like?
Loan processing:
From the initial consultation to post-settlement follow-ups, back-office support handles every administrative task, including compliance checks and lender requirements.

Client relationship management:

The back-office team serves as the primary client contact, ensuring clients receive timely updates, which keeps the broker free for high-level tasks.

Quality assurance:

Monthly reviews and staff training ensure that all files are kept in line with compliance standards.

Upskilled staff:

The team possesses Australian mortgage broking qualifications and stays updated on compliance and industry changes, acting as an extension of the broker's team.

Why this split works

The head broker bears most of the operational costs, including staffing, office expenses and training. In exchange, brokers receive high-level support that allows them to focus on high-value activities like closing deals and nurturing key client relationships. Brokers are likely to stay because the cost of replicating this set-up on their own would be significantly higher.

Model 2: Part-time support (16 hours)

Suggested commission split:
60/40 in favour of the head broker

For brokers who prefer a balance between autonomy and support, part-time back-office assistance provides flexibility during busy periods. This model works particularly well when brokers handle the majority of their tasks but need additional help during peak times or for specific aspects of loan processing.

Key aspects of part-time support

Selective loan processing:
The back-office team assists brokers with specific parts of the loan process, such as verifying documents, assisting with valuations or reviewing loan structures.

Compliance oversight:
Ensures that all loan applications meet the required standards and that all documentation is complete.

File health reviews:
These are periodic audits of loan files to ensure they are compliant with aggregator and lender standards.

Why this split works

Part-time support offers brokers a lifeline during their busiest periods but doesn't fully replace their involvement in the loan process. This model is cost-effective for brokers in regional areas or those with smaller deal sizes. The split reflects the value provided while leaving room for the broker to manage more of their business.

Model 3: Flexible support (8 hours)

Suggested commission split:
50/50 in favour of the broker

This model is perfect for newer brokers or those who prefer to handle most of the loan process independently but need limited administrative help. With only eight hours of support, the back-office team focuses on repetitive or time-consuming tasks, allowing brokers to streamline their workload while staying hands-on with their clients.

Key aspects of flexible support:

Document management:

The back-office team manages document renaming, splitting and uploads according to set aggregator requirements.

Data entry:
Entry of loan information into CRMs and spreadsheets, allowing brokers to focus on analysis and client engagement.

Back book analysis:
Helps brokers identify re-engagement opportunities from past clients, ensuring they can stay on top of potential refinancing opportunities.

Why this split works
For brokers who are newer or more hands-on, this model offers essential administrative support without taking away the majority of their responsibilities. It also incentivises brokers to stay longer as they build experience, knowing that they can eventually move up to higher support models as their business grows.

Conclusion

Strategic commission splits should reflect the level of back-office support provided. Brokers who receive full-spectrum support can justify a larger percentage going to the head broker, while those who are more independent will appreciate a 50/50 or 60/40 split. By offering these structured models, head brokers can create a set-up where brokers are less likely to leave because they're receiving invaluable support and are thriving within a well-established ecosystem.

Retention becomes less about locking brokers in and more about creating an environment that is hard to walk away from. With the right balance of support and commission structure, both the head broker and individual brokers can achieve their goals.

CHAPTER 33

Navigating contracts, contractor splits and broker agreements in mortgage broking

In the dynamic world of Australian mortgage broking, a broker's success is built not only on securing clients but also on establishing clear, well-structured contracts and agreements. From employment contracts to contractor commission splits, having everything documented provides legal protection, ensures smooth operations and avoids potential disputes.

Gina had always taken a laid-back approach to running her females-only mortgage business. Her team was tight-knit, composed of friends and colleagues she had known through industry events for years.

As business boomed, Gina hired Sara, a talented broker, to help manage her growing client base. Excited to bring her on board, Gina didn't think twice about drafting a proper contract. Over cocktails in the city, they shook hands and Gina used a generic employment template she found online, assuming it would cover everything.

For two years, things went well. Sara became a trusted face in the brokerage, handling some of Gina's top clients. Eventually, Sara's ambitions grew and so did her greed. Without a clear contract in place, Sara believed she had the right to charge the clients for meetings. She raised invoices without Gina's knowing. Soon, Gina caught wind and Sara resigned. Gina saw emails with invoices and realised Sara had pocketed over $20,000 in client fees. With nothing explicitly stated in Sara's contract about fees or what Sara could take as commissions, they were headed for a legal battle.

What followed was months of heated discussions, escalating to court. In the end, the court sided with Sara. Gina ended up paying hefty legal fees and lost not only key clients but also her faith in people. She decided to get out of broking and get into coaching instead.

People are your make or break. How you treat your team and employees has a follow-on effect on your clients. If it is only you, you may be tempted to casually run the operation like friends. This is the biggest mistake you can make. Attitude is everything. If you professionally onboard that one team member, it will set the culture of your firm.

Human resources is as expensive as in a big form, so many brokers do the basic payroll and leave in XERO. However, XERO does not have additional services like employment law advice, health and safety tools and disciplinary actions and grievances. Therefore, you do need to invest in an HR management software to manage your staff and avoid having to have those awkward conversations.

Whether you're a sole operator or managing a growing brokerage, understanding these key elements below is critical for long-term success.

Case study 1: Crafted and clean employment contracts

A prominent mortgage brokerage company in Sydney was experiencing operation inefficiencies due to lack of clarity in employment contracts. The company had both fulltime brokers and part-time client service managers. The challenge? Establishing division of roles and responsibilities. Support staff was uncertain of their roles relative to brokers, and that caused inefficiencies and unfulfilled expectations.

With clear employment contracts, the brokerage defined working hours, specific duties and provided clear expectations for compensation and benefits. This not only made their operations much smoother but also saved the business from potential legal fights due to unclear terms.

Takeaway:
Having clear outlines of job descriptions, working hours, roles and compensation on paper, in the form of employment contracts, can help ensure smooth sailing in day-to-day operations and prevent legal complications.

Case study 2: Need to document contractor splits

A mortgage broker in Melbourne hired more than 10 independent contractors to help meet an increase in demand. But while the business expanded, tracking commissions, particularly with closing dates of deals that varied widely, became a logistical headache. The payment system was a grey area, and contractors soon voiced their concerns with the cuts they were receiving.

The broker was then introduced to a detailed and transparent contractor split agreement. It laid out the specific percentages by origination, effort and deal type so that there was clarity on how commissions would be split. There was also a dispute resolution mechanism, which would help alleviate possible friction.

Takeaway:

In any commission-based business – in fact, in any business for that matter, but particularly true in brokerage activities such as mortgage broking – commission splits must be documented and agreed to. This promotes transparency, motivates everyone and develops trust in the team.

Case Study 3: Three trainer policies with a focus on brokers.

A Brisbane-based mortgage broker has discovered that all too many brokers and owners fail to put detailed broker's contracts in place. She employed a friend as a PAYG broker under a generic employment contract she discovered online. What she didn't realise is that the contract didn't cover critical areas such as ownership of clients, rights to trail commissions and client fees.

Her friend, after two years, wanted to be independent. Not only did she want to take the clients she worked with but the trail commissions from those clients as well. The standard clauses around ownership of clients and trail commissions left the head broker with little legal ground to stand on. The case reached court, and the head broker lost and owed big legal fees and a settlement.

Takeaway:

When you hire brokers, a generic contract won't suffice. Use a specialised lawyer when writing contracts, which should specifically cover the mortgage broking industry, detailing ownership of clients, trail commissions and client fee policies.

Essential components of every mortgage broking agreement

Client ownership: Clearly lay out who owns the client relationship and whether the broker can take clients with him when he leaves the business.

Trail provisions: Specify the treatment of trail commissions both during and after employment.

Broker compensation: Specify how to pay brokers, commission percentages, bonuses and other incentives.

Non-compete clauses: Prevent brokers from quickly starting a competing business in the same geographic area or from raiding their clients when they leave.

Clawbacks: Discuss how clawbacks will be treated if a loan is refinanced or discharged in a certain time frame.

Conclusion

The cases above clearly teach one crucial lesson in the business of mortgage broking – well-documented contracts and agreements are pivotal. They safeguard the brokerage as well as the brokers, keep things moving smoothly and avoid the potential for legal disputes later on.

If you're a head broker, leave nothing to chance. Always review and renew your contracts on a regular basis and get sound professional advice specifically related to the mortgage industry. Implementing these practices will leave you better protected in the long run while developing stronger relationships among your team and creating a place to work and grow in your brokerage.

CHAPTER 34

Unlocking the potential: Why hiring experienced brokers after selling their businesses can transform your brokerage

Mortgage broking is a lucrative career, with young brokers often rising to success quickly, scaling their brokerages and investing in ventures beyond finance. As they grow, younger brokers may tend to overlook the value of hiring mature and experienced brokers, assuming they'll slow down the fast pace or challenge the existing dynamics. Yet, integrating these seasoned professionals can unlock significant growth potential.

This chapter explores the reasons why younger mortgage brokers should actively seek out experienced brokers who have sold their businesses and how to successfully integrate them.

What do mature brokers want?

When brokers sell their trail books or step back from ownership, they often aren't looking to dive back into the grind. Understanding their needs is crucial to building a mutually beneficial relationship.

- **More free time:** They want the flexibility to pursue other interests.

- **Less pressure:** They are not looking to carry the weight of ownership or entrepreneurship again.

- **Fair financial reward:** They want to be paid well for their skills and experience without the stress of building a business from the ground up.

The case for experience

Mortgage brokers with decades of experience are also nimble client managers and deeply knowledgeable about the expansion – peak – contraction and trough cycle-specific market drivers. They have faced all sorts of economic cycles and hurdles many times over. They have adapted and emerged stronger from changes. Therefore, when these seasoned professionals come on board at a young brokerage, they lend it credibility, a wide network of contacts and a proven ability to navigate complex financial situations. Mature brokers enhance the profile of a younger brokerage and bring clients the best of both worlds by combining fresh ideas with their tested strategies.

Techniques for successful merging

1. Physical presence (meeting space)

Veteran brokers do things the old-fashioned way. They prefer personal contact and like to meet in person. Younger brokers can schedule regular meetings with them at the office. During these catch-ups, the whole team assembles to share their own experiences with the rest. Monthly or weekly team meetings, in which more seasoned brokers review through incidents that have happened, offer those younger at the business their nuggets of knowledge that they have gleaned from their experiences. This can also cover a multitude of successes and failings.

2. Leverage networks

Over the years, veteran brokers have built innumerable contacts and relationships, most of which have been cultivated through trust and successful transactions. These include real estate agents, financial planners and generations of clients. This network is something younger brokers can leverage to grow their own client base.

These mature brokers are also ideal for business development and sales roles, where their established presence and reputation can more readily generate leads than a more junior broker might. A principal can leverage these connections to generate leads and set up specific lead-generation targets for these mature brokers. That way, you play to their strengths and they do not feel burdened by administrative tasks.

3. Mentorship opportunities

Seasoned brokers, having seen the peaks and valleys of this industry, can guide younger brokers beyond theory. Create mentorship programs that allow junior brokers to shadow and learn nuances in client management, loan structuring and navigating regulatory changes from experienced professionals. Nothing will replace this knowledge transfer, and it's a way for seasoned pros to impart their hard-won lessons to build legacy. This inculcates an environment of mutual respect where seasoned brokers feel their experience is appreciated whilst younger brokers receive real-time mentoring.

4. Train with technology

All newcomers may struggle with anything new, whilst experienced brokers are often fast to learn new technologies with appropriate training – provided they are willing and eager. Most often, the power of personal and pace-appropriate training is overlooked. Mature brokers need to be convinced why taking on something new is worth their time. One should emphasize how new tools streamline their jobs and make their workflow easier. Expect the resistance, listen to pain points and provide effective technology solutions to these brokers. Initially, there might be some pushback, but with patience and persistence their aversion to using digital tools can be broken.

5. Strategic time management

Mature brokers might not feel like chained to an office for eight hours at this stage of their career, so their experience can be strategically leveraged. A way to leverage their skills without bogging them down with administrative roles is to utilise them more at networking events or high-profile client meetings. Brief them so that they can take the stage and impart their unique case scenarios through storytelling. Brokers with huge brokerages and high number of clients might hire admin staff so they can focus on high-ticket, revenue-generating activities while younger brokers or admin staff manage their everyday processes themselves.

Conclusion

The mature brokers bring wisdom and strategy into a younger, tech-forward brokerage. Younger brokers can maximise the full potential of these seasoned professionals by valuing their experience and tailoring roles to meet their needs. Whether through mentorship, business development and 'signature talks', the contributions made by more seasoned brokers can completely change a brokerage for the better – the best of both worlds as trusted relationships merge with new-age growth strategies.

Recap of Section 4: Building, expanding and scaling your brokerage

Chapter 29: Scaling smart: When and how to add staff

- Assess workload vs. revenue, and identify signs of burnout or missed opportunities.

- Project cash flows before hiring, ensuring revenue supports the extra overheads.

- Write job descriptions for brokers, support staff and operations managers to ensure efficient role allocation.

- Start with part-time support or an offshore assistant for administrative tasks without overextending financially.

Chapter 30: Building a sales-driven culture

- Train all staff to focus on building relationships right from the first client interaction.

- Develop sales skills across every role and practice upselling services.

- Hold weekly meetings where all team members share insights on client success stories.

- Establish performance metrics to track the impact of each role in the sales process.

Chapter 31: Mastering mentorship

- Mentorship should be tailored as per the needs – compliance, growth strategy or technical skills-related.

- Develop a structured mentorship plan with measurable outcomes.

- Leverage multiple sources like FBAA and MFAA while also considering private coaches.

- Set aside time for peer networking and attending lender-specific training sessions.

Chapter 32: Tailored commission splits and support models

- Implement tiered commission structures depending on the broker's experience, workload and level of support required.

- Ensure brokers receiving higher back-office support have a lower split, while independent brokers retain more commission for handling their own client work.

- Analyse the profitability, ensuring the commission splits sustain both business growth and broker retention.

- Clearly communicate the support and responsibilities tied to each commission structure.

Chapter 33: Navigating contracts and broker agreements

- Work with a lawyer to create detailed broker agreements that cover client ownership, commission splits and trail commission policies.

- Incorporate non-compete clauses to protect your business from brokers leaving and setting up nearby or poaching clients.

- Ensure contracts include clear procedures for handling commission disputes, preventing potential legal battles.

- Review and update contracts annually to ensure compliance with changing employment laws.

Chapter 34: Hiring experienced brokers after selling their businesses

- Offer experienced brokers roles focusing on business development or mentoring junior brokers.

- Allow seasoned brokers to utilise their existing relationships for lead generation.

- Pair experienced brokers with junior brokers to facilitate knowledge transfer, focusing on complex deal structures and client management.

- Provide tech training to experienced brokers, showing how new tools can ease their workflow without overwhelming them.

CHAPTER 35

Prepping for a prosperous new year: Year-end essentials for mortgage brokers

The end of the calendar year and the first couple of months of the new year are often a quiet period for mortgage brokers, making it the perfect time to get your house in order and set yourself up for a strong start whenever you step into a new year.

Whether you're a seasoned broker or just starting out, there are some key financial and operational strategies you should focus on before the year wraps up. Let's dive into some simple, practical steps that will help you manage debt, protect your assets and optimise your tax situation for the year ahead.

1. Manage your debit loans

As a mortgage broker, you know the importance of managing debt better than anyone. Debit loans refer to the liabilities or borrowings that you or your business owes, and it's essential to keep these loans under control to maintain a healthy financial standing. Review any outstanding loans, and assess whether refinancing or adjusting repayment plans could help you save on interest or reduce your debt load.

Tip: Use the end-of-year period to get a clear picture of your current liabilities. Take stock of upcoming repayments, interest rates and any changes in your financial obligations for the next year.

---

2. Set up a company for asset protection

Incorporating your business can offer you asset protection by shielding personal assets from potential business liabilities. Plus, operating as a company allows you to benefit from the corporate tax rate, which is often lower than individual tax rates.

For example, if your personal income puts you in a high tax bracket, it might make sense to distribute some of your earnings through a corporate structure, potentially lowering your tax bill (refer to Chapter 26 on bucket companies). Make sure you talk to your accountant to see if this strategy suits your business and personal circumstances.

3. Review and adjust for year-end

As the year comes to an end, now is the time to do a comprehensive review of your business. Here's a checklist of essential tasks for the end of the year:

Reconnect with your accountant: Book a session for February of the next year to discuss your finances. Consider inviting them to your Christmas or year-end party along with potential referrers. Accountants can be a valuable source of referrals.

Task your bookkeeper: Ensure your GST is lodged quarterly and all your accounts are up to date by the first week of every month. Set up calendar reminders to stay on track.

Quarterly tax planning: Meet with your accountant now to review current tax breaks and optimise your deductions for the year ahead. For example, before purchasing a trail book, your accountant can help you explore strategies like depreciation through another entity, which could help with tax optimisation.

4. Keep tax obligations covered

Open a second business bank account to set aside funds for tax obligations. Direct 40% of your income into this account and use any surplus to reduce personal, non-deductible debts by transferring the money into an offset account. Over time, this can significantly reduce your interest costs.

Tip: Keeping your tax funds separate ensures you won't be caught off guard when it's time to pay, and it's a smart way to optimise your banking strategy for long-term savings.

5. Stay on top of your cash flow

Ensure you're using accounting software like XERO, MYOB, QuickBooks or SAGE to categorise your expenses and track your revenue. A well-structured chart of accounts will give you a clear picture of where your money is going and help you make informed financial decisions for the year.

Pro Tip: Implementing a structured accounting system can help you project your cash flow needs more accurately and reduce the risk of overspending.

6. Review insurance and estate planning

Now is also a good time to review your business insurance, estate planning and wills to make sure they reflect your current situation and future goals. Changes in your personal or business life like new assets, children or a change in your relationship status can impact your insurance and estate planning needs.

For instance, you don't want to leave your insurance payout going to an ex-spouse or have outdated beneficiaries in your will. Make sure everything is up to date to avoid any unpleasant surprises.

Conclusion

The end of the year is the perfect opportunity to reflect on the past 12 months, plan for the future and take the strategic steps needed to optimise your business. By staying on top of your debt, protecting your assets, setting up tax strategies and preparing your accounting systems, you can head into the next year with confidence.

Remember, your financial health as a mortgage broker is just as important as the work you do for your clients. Use this time wisely, and you'll set yourself up for a prosperous and successful new year and the years ahead.

CHAPTER 36

Benchmarking: The secret to staying ahead in mortgage broking

Sean had always been a standout performer during COVID and the low interest rate landscape. After thirteen interest rate increases, reality started creeping in. His income plateaued, the leads trickled in slower than he expected, and he was stretched thin looking after all the clients he had acquired.

Sean found himself staring at his spreadsheet with numbers that didn't make sense. His revenue was nowhere near where he thought it would be, he had no idea how his expenses compared to other brokers or whether he was spending too much on marketing. Sean had no idea if he was doing something wrong or if this was just what life as a self-employed broker looked like.

The next day, at a lender coffee cluster, Sean confided in a colleague who had been in the business for years. This broker, Sam, listened carefully, then smiled knowingly.

'Sean,' Sam said, 'I know you don't want your aggregator knowing everything about you. You can confidentially compare your financials with others.'

Sean had heard the term mentioned before by his aggregator's sales team but never thought much about it. Sam explained how benchmarking had transformed his own brokerage. By comparing key performance metrics like revenue per deal, client retention rates and marketing spend, Sam had gained clarity on where he was falling behind and what he needed to change.

Sam said, 'You wouldn't run a race without knowing where the finish line is, right? You're just running blind. Benchmarking tells you how far ahead or behind you are compared to other brokers similar to you so you can make the right moves to catch up or stay ahead.'

Sean decided to give it a try. He joined a peer benchmarking group within his franchise. At the next profit meeting, they all laid their numbers on the table. Sean's jaw dropped. One broker, who had been in the business the same amount of time as him, was pulling in double the revenue with far fewer expenses. Another broker had bundled their subscriptions, and the costs were a fraction of Sean's, while other brokers were thriving in coworking spaces or fully remote set-ups. Armed with this new data, Sean took action. Within six months, Sean saw a 25% increase in revenue, his client retention stabilised and he felt more supported.

When you work in a bank or a corporate environment, targets and goals are set for you. Managers keep a close eye on your performance, offer guidance and push you to achieve more. But when you go self-employed as a mortgage broker, the tables turn. You become your own manager setting your goals, staying motivated and pushing yourself to improve. Without that external pressure, it's easy to lose focus or get complacent, and that's where benchmarking comes in. Benchmarking is a powerful tool that helps brokers measure their business against others, ensuring they stay competitive, motivated and on the path to success.

You will attend peer-to-peer sessions. You will exchange ideas with other brokers. Brokerage business owners will share ideas and plans with you, but no one will discuss their businesses' financial performance with you in specific dollar terms. In those instances, how can you compare yourself and truly gauge how you are doing? Yes, you are running your own race, but are you running in the right direction like the other brokers you look up to?

Let's break down why benchmarking is essential for brokers, especially if you're part of a franchise group.

1. Performance improvement: See where you stand, improve where you can

The first benefit of benchmarking is understanding your financial performance compared to other brokers in your franchise group. By analysing key financial ratios, revenue figures and costs, you get a clear picture of where your business stands.

For example, if you see that other brokers with similar years in business are generating higher revenue, you can analyse their ideal types, client mix or marketing strategies to adjust your approach. This way, benchmarking pushes you to continuously improve by setting realistic goals based on hard data.

Tip: Look at the profit margins, number of deals and the costs of the top brokers in your network. By comparing these numbers to your own, you can pinpoint areas to focus on for improvement.

---

2. Strategic decision-making: Get data-driven insights for growth

Being a mortgage broker means making a lot of strategic decisions. Should you hire more staff? Invest in marketing? Move into a bigger office?

Benchmarking gives you the data to make informed choices rather than relying on guesswork. For instance, if top brokers in your group spend a set percentage on marketing and consistently outperform the competition, you can adjust your marketing budget to match, ensuring you're not underspending or wasting resources.

With real-time benchmarking data, you can see where successful brokers are spending their money and where they're cutting costs. This ensures that your investments in staff, office space or marketing pay off rather than becoming unnecessary overheads.

3. Using data: Set financial KPIs that motivate

Benchmarking helps you see what's possible. By benchmarking your performance against others in the brokerage industry, you can establish difficult yet feasible KPIs. By this application, when you see a number one business owner build their business rate to $500,000 in top-line income over seven years, it tells you that your goal of reaching that dollar amount in five years is an actualist one.

Use this data to establish KPIs that drive you to achieve similar or even better results. And these data-driven KPIs provide the hard numbers to shoot for, with the assurance to take your business to the next level, hire more staff or enter new markets.

4. Cost efficiency: Slash unnecessary expenses

One of the fastest ways to improve your operating profits is by cutting unnecessary costs. Benchmarking helps you compare your outgoings to other brokers and identify where your money is leaking – whether that's in unused software, overhead costs or outdated technology. Reducing these expenses boosts your profitability without needing to increase revenue.

For example, if you're paying high rent for an office space that's larger than necessary, benchmarking can reveal that other brokers are using coworking spaces or working remotely to cut costs. This simple adjustment can boost profitability immediately.

5. Operational efficiency: Use proven business models

Franchise groups often have a proven business model, which means brokers in these groups share best practices, standardised processes and consistent training. By benchmarking against this proven model, you're more likely to see results because you know the strategy works.

If your franchise group has a CRM or marketing platform that others are using to achieve success, benchmark your usage of these tools. Are you using all the features? Have you optimised your process? This approach to benchmarking keeps you from leaving growth levers unpulled. Commission structures and CRM tools tied to a standard chart of accounts give you access to benchmarking that identifies the holes in your business and best practices to follow in running your operations efficiently.

6. Working together and motivating: Good competitive phases of supporting each other

Benchmarking strengthens your business and your franchise group as a whole. When everyone is benchmarking, trying to be better, it's a rising tide that lifts all boats. By seeing how well others are doing, it fosters healthy competition and encourages you to drive harder. It also presents opportunities to share successes and learnings.

Conclusion

For mortgage brokers (and particularly franchise group brokers), benchmarking is a game-changer. It's not only about comparing things; it's about having access to data to remain competitive, make better decisions and boost performance. If you embrace this mindset, you can propel your business to new levels, eliminate frivolous spending and build systematic growth.

CHAPTER 37

Maximising the value of trail commissions in your mortgage brokerage

When you hear a broker downplay the importance of trail commissions, you know they're missing the bigger picture. Trail commissions are the most valuable asset a mortgage broker holds. Some brokers focus on building it but don't know how to use it to its full potential when it gets to certain dollars per month. Say your trail does get to $25,000 a month, what do you intend to do then? Eat the principal, or use it to diversify your investments?

The overwhelming demand to buy trail books proves this with 85% of brokers looking to acquire trail books right now. Understanding how to strategically allocate and use trail commissions can make the difference between surviving and thriving as a mortgage broker.

So, how do you allocate your trail income to maximise growth and maintain a balanced brokerage?

The concept of trail allocation

Think of your commissions like how you advise clients to use their offset accounts – it's a tool for managing expenses and saving for a rainy day. Similarly, splitting your trail and upfront commissions strategically can help manage fixed expenses, create a profit buffer and fund future growth.

Should you use trail commissions to cover fixed costs?

The strategy depends on where your business is in its lifecycle. Upfront commissions provide an immediate cash flow boost. For a newer brokerage, covering fixed expenses with trail commissions can help manage early financial instability – bear in mind, I don't mean that when the trail is a few hundred dollars a month. We are talking of when your business grows and brings in at least $4,000 to $5,000 a month in trail. That is the time it's smarter to shift fixed costs to upfront commissions using trail commissions to build reserves, invest in marketing or even explore new opportunities.

The reasoning is that new brokerages have lower costs compared to a growing business who will spend to expand. Also, you want to stay hungry and driven at the start and not squirrel away your small trail payments to get the false sense of security.

Let's break this down into two scenarios.

Scenario 1: Trail commission of $12,000 per month

At this level, your focus is on maintaining stability and managing expenses with precision. Here's how you could allocate your trail income:

1. Rent or coworking space

Start small, especially if you're in a growth phase. Choose a modest office or coworking space to minimise overhead while still having a professional environment.

2. Subscriptions and tools

Tools like CoreLogic, Trello and XERO are essential for day-to-day operations. Set aside enough of your trail to cover these monthly subscriptions, as they are critical to business functionality.

3. Outsourced staff

Many brokers rely on virtual assistants or offshore teams. Your trail should ensure these staff are paid consistently and incentivised to remain loyal.

The savings from offshore staff compared to onshore personnel can be reinvested into growing your business.

4. Marketing and advertising

You may not be able to afford large-scale campaigns yet, but you can still run cost-effective digital marketing strategies. Focus on social media presence and local digital ads to keep your name top of mind with potential clients.

5. Emergency fund

Even in the early stages, set aside a percentage of your trail income for an emergency fund. This will provide a buffer for months when income from upfront commissions fluctuates.

Scenario 2: Trail commission of $25,000 per month

With a higher trail, you have more room to expand and take calculated risks. Here's how to allocate effectively at this income level:

1. Purchase office space

Consider using your SMSF to purchase an office. This not only diversifies your business assets but can also turn a major cost into a profit centre by renting out desks or spaces within your office.

2. Hiring and expanding the team

With a higher trail, you can afford to hire a credit analyst, onshore brokers or a personal assistant to help you scale without risking burnout. This reduces keyman risk and allows for consistent service levels even as you grow.

3. Enhanced marketing

At this stage, you can invest in professional marketing services, a high-end website and more sophisticated video production to attract new clients. Running referral competitions or offering client incentives will also help build loyalty and attract new business.

4. Professional development

Set aside part of your trail for training and upskilling both yourself and your team. Invest in leadership courses or workshops to keep your team motivated and aligned with your vision for the business.

5. Building a larger emergency fund

A larger business needs a more substantial buffer to cover unexpected costs, especially if you want the freedom to take time off or invest in new ventures. Building a robust emergency fund will give you the security to take calculated risks without putting the business at risk.

6. Negotiation power with lenders

Once you're earning significant trail income, you can leverage this to negotiate better deals with lenders, securing higher commissions or exclusive deals that can further boost your income.

Conclusion

Success in mortgage broking goes beyond settlements. It's about mastering the discipline on how to use both upfront and trail income resources at your disposal to build a business that grows year on year. Whether you're earning $12,000 or $25,000 in trail commissions per month, how you allocate these funds can make or break your business. The most successful mortgage brokers aren't just great at closing deals, they're savvy business owners who know how to reinvest in their business, manage costs and plan for the future. They aren't living on a day-to-day basis but have bigger visions.

Trail income should never be seen as an afterthought or just passive income. Instead, it should be used to build, expand and protect the longevity and value of your brokerage.

CHAPTER 38

Protecting your mortgage brokerage: Five essential insurance policies to reduce risk

One day, Luigi received an urgent phone call. His laptop had been hacked and a large portion of his client data that he saved in a folder on the drive had been compromised. Sensitive information, including tax file numbers and financial details, was leaked. The news spread quickly and clients began withdrawing their business out of fear. Luigi was hit hard with investigations from his aggregator and by the legal fees and damage control required to fix the mess.

After the incident, Luigi was faced with a mountain of expenses to prove he was innocent and go into damage control. He hired cybersecurity experts, bought legal advice and worked to save his reputation. If he had purchased cyber insurance, he would not have been under so much stress. He travelled the country, doing roadshows to tell other brokers what had happened to him. While sharing was painful, he collaborated with us to help prevent other brokers from treating cyber threats lightly.

If you're a mortgage broking business, you're going to want to ensure that you have the right suite of insurance policies to protect your business for the long term. I was speaking with a broker team in South Australia the other day. They shared their budget for yearly insurances, which totalled a whopping $40,000 per year. Although this might seem like a significant cost, it emphasises the importance of insurance in protecting their business. For brokers, writing the correct policies can safeguard cash flow and bridge business continuity during an unforeseen event.

In this chapter, we will explore the five policies all mortgage brokers should have. They can protect your brokerage from risks and costs, as real-world examples demonstrate.

1. Key man insurance

Samuel and Nicholas (both partners at Suga Brokers) had the foresight to take out key man insurance. When Samuel had a bad skiing accident that left him unable to work for months, the firm was losing a lot of money. The insurance payout was used to bring in temporary support for the business and retrain team members to take over Samuel's duties. It also reassured wealthy clients that the firm was capable of handling their deals without delay.

Key benefits:
This type of insurance ensures business continuity when a critical team member is unable to work. The payout can help cover the loss in revenue, the cost of hiring replacements or additional training to keep things running smoothly.

2. Buy–sell insurance

AJ and PK co-owned A Grade Mortgage Brokers. When PK tragically passed away, his share of the business was left to his daughter, who had no interest in mortgage broking. Thankfully, they had buy–sell insurance which allowed AJ to purchase PK's share from his estate. This helped maintain control of the business and provided PK's family with fair compensation.

Key benefits:

This policy guarantees the business remains in capable hands while also providing fair compensation to the deceased partner's family. It helps avoid complications that can arise when a partner's share of the business passes to someone without the skills or interest in mortgage broking.

3. Professional indemnity insurance

B.I.D. Mortgages employed a new PAYG broker who made an error by not informing a client about early exit fees when refinancing a loan. The client was furious and sued the brokerage for negligence. Luckily, B.I.D. Mortgages had PI insurance that took care of both the legal fees and compensation to the client, thus sparing the brokerage with an irrecoverable financial hit.

Key benefits:

Professional indemnity insurance covers your business in case of legal action due to advice you give that results in negligence or mistakes. It serves as a buffer against legal fees and compensation, protecting your cash flow against unexpected legal encounters.

4. Public liability insurance

F2F Home Loans holds all client meetings in their physical office. One rainy day, a client slipped on a wet floor and sustained an injury. The client sued F2F for negligence. With public liability insurance, the firm covered the legal costs and compensation, avoiding a costly financial hit.

Key benefits:
If your business operates from a physical location or interacts with clients face-to-face, public liability insurance covers injuries or accidents that occur on your premises, reducing the risk of costly lawsuits.

5. Cyber insurance

Most mortgage brokers, including Digi Wigi Loan Advisors, keep client data in digital form. Digi Wigi also faced legal and reputational damage when a cyber attack leaked sensitive client information like tax file numbers. Fortunately, their cyber insurance policy covered the expense of the breach investigation, legal expenses, client notification and even reputation management services.

Key benefits:
As the world becomes more digitised, so too does cyber insurance. It assists you in dealing with the

aftermath of data breaches that cost you legal fees, client compensation and rebuilding your brand's reputation.

Conclusion

I agree this is a subject that, more often than not, most mortgage brokers would like to avoid. So, I saved this for the end, but it is a necessary evil. In the mortgage broking industry, it's better to be safe than sorry, and these five important insurance policies will assist you in reducing risk and ensuring your brokerage sustains no matter what.

Such policies act as fiscal insurance, allowing your brokerage to persevere through unforeseen obstacles without immense financial loss. The price of insurance may change over the years, but make sure that you regularly review and update your policies with a competent risk adviser.

With these insurances embedded into your brokerage, you can grow your business trustingly without worrying about the common risks that would slow you down.

Action steps

- Take stock of your existing insurance protection.

- Engage a qualified risk adviser to ensure your brokerage is sufficiently protected.

- Include these critical insurances in your business's long-term growth plan.

Recap of Section 5: Practical advice for managing day-to-day operations

Chapter 35: Year-end essentials for mortgage brokers

- Manage debit loans, reduce debt costs and optimise repayment plans.

- Set up a company to protect personal assets and benefit from corporate tax rates.

- Engage with your accountant for tax planning, and task your bookkeeper to lodge your returns on time.

- Open a second business account and direct 40% of income to cover tax liabilities.

- Use XERO, MYOB or QuickBooks accounting software to categorise expenses and forecast cash flow needs.

- Ensure your business insurances and estate plans reflect changes in assets, personal circumstances and beneficiaries.

Chapter 36: Benchmarking

- Compare key financial metrics and use benchmarking data to make informed decisions

- Set financial KPIs using benchmarking to set ambitious yet achievable performance goals for your brokerage.

- Compare overhead costs, streamline expenses and leverage tools used by top brokers in your network.

- Engage in peer benchmarking groups to foster healthy competition and continuous improvement.

Chapter 37: Maximising the value of trail commissions in your mortgage brokerage

- Use trail commissions to cover fixed costs as the business grows.

- Set aside a portion of trail income to create a financial buffer for slow months.

- As trail income increases, invest in marketing, office space (through SMSF) or new hires to expand the business.

- Use higher trail income to negotiate better commissions or exclusive deals with lenders.

- Allocate funds from trail income for team training and personal upskilling

Chapter 38: Protecting your mortgage brokerage

- Protect your brokerage from revenue loss by insuring critical team members.

- Protect ownership transitions in case of a partner's death, securing your business continuity.

- Safeguard against client claims of negligence or errors in service.

- Protect your brokerage from claims related to client injuries or accidents occurring on business premises.

- Protect your brokerage from data breaches, cyber attacks and reputational costs.

Afterword

This handbook is not just another handbook that recycles basic tips and glosses over the hard-hitting topics. It breaks down both the fundamentals and the advanced tactics for brokers like yourself, who are transitioning from a salesperson to a multifaceted business owner.

Mortgage broking is not a zero-sum game. If the industry is to survive, the numbers need to grow. This will only happen if mortgage brokers find success. In 2024, less than 10% of mortgage brokers make more than $150,000 in revenue as self-employed business owners. I have repeated myself and emphasised on the most important themes over and over again. This was deliberately done to make it stick with you. As you finish this book, I hope it serves as both a guide and a reminder that every successful mortgage broker in that 10% started from the same place with an overwhelming desire to succeed but not always knowing how.

Whether you're transitioning from PAYG to self-employment, trying to maximise your trail book or looking to future-proof your business finances, this book equips you with the tools to succeed.

I encourage you to continue learning, stay adaptable and, most importantly, never lose sight of the bigger picture – helping your clients achieve their financial goals. This is more than a read, it is an investment into your future tailored to your career growth.

About the Author – Natasha Menon

Industry Insider | Mortgage Broker Growth Strategist | Financial Performance Expert

Natasha Menon has more than 15 years' experience in financial services working with some of the most successful professionals in the field – accountants, superannuation advisers, SMSF experts, retirement planners, financial planners, wealth managers and, most importantly, mortgage brokers. Natasha has been at the forefront of mortgage broker business success, working with brokers across various service plans and gaining unparalleled access to the inner workings of high-performing brokerage firms. Her expertise extends beyond the surface. She has:

☑ Shadowed top decision-makers, attending confidential meetings and analysing financial data from mortgage brokers of all sizes.

☑ Worked closely with the most profitable broker business owners uncovering what truly drives growth, sustainability and long-term profitability.

☑ Served as the only Broker Business Performance Analyst within the Profit team gaining deep insights into trail book buying & selling and understanding the financial challenges brokers face at every stage of their journey.

Natasha is on a mission to arm new to mid-sized mortgage broker business owners with the insights, strategies and foresight they need to scale their businesses, maximise their profitability and future-proof their success.

Speaker Bio

Natasha Menon is a seasoned business analyst in mortgage broking, business performance analysis and profitability strategies. As an adored LinkedIn newsletter writer, she shares practical, actionable advice for brokers looking to increase profitability, improve business performance and stay ahead in an increasingly competitive market to give all brokers not just motivation but a framework to work off and create a proper path to success.

Notes

www.ingramcontent.com/pod-product-compliance
Lightning Source LLC
Chambersburg PA
CBHW040914210326
41597CB00030B/5076